FLEA MARKET

STYLE

DECORATING + DISPLAYING + COLLECTING

A **Better Homes and Gardens** Book
An Imprint of
HMH

Published by:
Houghton Mifflin Harcourt
Boston • New York
www.hmhco.com

For information about permission to reproduce selections from this book, write to trade.permissions@hmhco.com or to Permissions, Houghton Mifflin Harcourt Publishing Company, 3 Park Avenue, 19th Floor, New York, New York 10016.

The publisher and author make no representations or warranties with respect to the accuracy or completeness of the contents of this work and specifically disclaim all warranties, including without limitation warranties of fitness for a particular purpose. No warranty may be created or extended by sales or promotional materials. The advice and strategies contained herein may not be suitable for every situation. This work is sold with the understanding that the publisher is not engaged in rendering legal, accounting, or other professional services. If professional assistance is required, the services of a competent professional person should be sought. Neither the publisher nor the author shall be liable for damages arising here from. The fact that an organization or Website is referred to in this work as a citation and/or a potential source of further information does not mean that the author or the publisher endorses the information the organization or Website may provide or recommendations it may take. Further, readers should be aware that Websites listed in this work may have changed or disappeared between when this work was written and when it is read.

TRADEMARKS: All trademarks are the property of their respective owners. Houghton Mifflin Harcourt is not associated with any product or vendor mentioned in this book.

Library of Congress Cataloging in Publication Data is available.
ISBN: 978-0-544-93187-9 (pbk); 978-0-544-93179-4 (ebk)
Printed in China
C&C 10 9 8 7 6 5 4 3 2 1

NOTE TO THE READERS: Due to differing conditions, tools, and individual skills, Houghton Mifflin Harcourt assumes no responsibility for any damages, injuries suffered, or losses incurred as a result of following the information published in this book. Before beginning any project, review the instructions carefully, and if any doubts or questions remain, consult local experts or authorities. Because codes and regulations vary greatly, you always should check with authorities to ensure that your project complies with all applicable local codes and regulations. Always read and observe all of the safety precautions provided by manufacturers of any tools, equipment, or supplies, and follow all accepted safety procedures.

BETTER HOMES AND GARDENS® FLEA MARKET STYLE

Senior Editor: Samantha S. Thorpe
Assistant Art Director: Christy Brokens
Contributing Editor: Pamela Porter
Contributing Designer: Stacey Willey
Contributing Copy Editor: Nancy Dietz
Cover Photographer: Edmund Barr
Cover Designer: Karen Reinecke

SPECIAL INTEREST PUBLICATIONS

Editorial Director: Jennifer Dorland Darling
Senior Art Director: Stephanie Hunter

BETTER HOMES AND GARDENS® MAGAZINE

Editor in Chief: Stephen Orr
Creative Director: Jennifer D. Madara
Editorial Director, Digital Content and Products: Jill Waage

HOUGHTON MIFFLIN HARCOURT

Editorial Director: Cindy Kitchel
Executive Editor, Brands: Anne Ficklen
Managing Editor: Marina Padakis Lowry
Art Director: Tai Blanche
Senior Production Coordinator: Kimberly Kiefer
Production Director: Tom Hyland
Production Editor: Donna Wright

CONTRIBUTING PHOTOGRAPHERS

Edmund Barr, John Bessler, Kim Cornelison, Reed Davis, Jacob Fox, Ed Gohlich, Jeff Herr, Mark Lohman, Anthony-Masterson, Rebekah Molloy, Kevin J. Miyazaki/Redux, Michael Partenio, David Tsay, Jay Wilde, Brie Williams.

CONTRIBUTING DESIGNERS, STYLISTS, & WRITERS

Tara Okerstrom-Bauer, Mara Boo, Christine Hofmann-Bourque, Karin Lidbeck-Brent, Andrea Caughey, Sarah Egge, Debra Engle, Anna Forkum, Jody Garlock, Jessica Brinkert Holtam, Lacey Howard, Laura Hull, Amy Jacobs, Jody Kennedy, Jennifer Kopf, Trevor Meers, Jenny O'Connor, Fifi O'Neil, Pamela Porter, Karen Reinecke, Eddie Ross, Margaret Zainey Roux, Carol Schalla, Linda Joan Smith, Donna Talley, Stacey Willey, Ann Wilson, Jennifer Wilson, Sarah Wolf.

Special Thanks to Vintage & Made Fair—Des Moines, Iowa

WELCOME
FLEA MARKET LOVERS

Thrifting, fleaing, junking, rummaging—whatever you call it, discovering and decorating with secondhand finds is a phenomenon that's here to stay. Why? Because the flea market approach results in personal, one-of-a-kind interiors and weaves seamlessly into any decorating style or budget. While no decorating degree is required, this thrifty, do-it-yourself method does call for patience, a sense of style, and a keen eye that knows when to reimagine an object and when to walk away. The following pages share practical tips and advice for shopping flea markets, home tours that illustrate how to work vintage finds into interiors of various styles, and ideas to inspire fun collections and delightful displays. The last section reveals how found objects can be repurposed into unique home accents. We're glad you're here!

Go. Seek. Flea happy.

CONTENTS

BOHEMIAN
HOMES
20

COTTAGE
HOMES
50

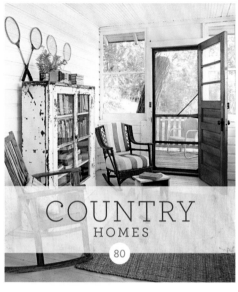

COUNTRY
HOMES
80

ROMANTIC
HOMES
110

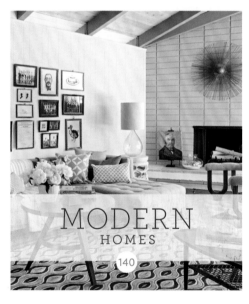

MODERN
HOMES
140

PROJECTS
FOR YOUR HOME
170

One-of-a-kind finds

Made in the shade

Man's best friend

Repurpose

FLEA MARKET
GUIDE

Whether you're heading across town or across the country, start your flea market adventure on the right foot—beginning, of course, with comfortable shoes! A little planning on the front end will pay off in spades, so do a little homework before hitting the road.

getting started
DECORATING WITH FLEA MARKET FINDS

Flea market style is all about you. It's about your passion to shop for vintage items and your vision to mix them into your home. It's decorating to express your personality in a nostalgic and creative way. It's more than a decorating style—it's a lifestyle.

KNOW YOUR STYLE Whether you favor modern interiors, down-home country style, or an eclectic mix, flea market decorating can work for you. Both versatile and timeless, vintage objects have a unique way of melding with any interior. Curating your look will take persistence and patience, though, and you'll likely make mistakes along the way. But given the nature of thrifting, they're not likely to be costly ones. Defining and sticking to a color palette is one key to success. Another is following your intuition and buying what you love. Only then will you be truly happy with your look. So hit the road at dawn, dig, explore, bargain, buy, and compose until you've created just the atmosphere you're seeking.

GET INSPIRED If you need help getting started with secondhand style or have found yourself in a rut, a little inspiration goes a long way in helping flea market newbies define their decorating style and helping veterans refine or rethink theirs. Scour home interiors books, magazines, blogs, and online idea boards regularly. Exciting new decorating ideas emerge daily, and discovering new trends or unique objects early in the game means you'll be prepared to snatch them up before someone else does. The more inspiration you seek, the more you'll discover what you like and don't like, and along the way you'll gain more confidence in your purchases and your personal decorating technique.

IMAGINE THE POSSIBILITIES If your weekend isn't complete without hitting a tag sale, and the anticipation of discovering a vintage treasure sends your heart aflutter, the flea market lifestyle is calling you. Now you need to develop the knack for envisioning old things in a new way—repurposing, restyling, reimagining, remaking. One of the most exciting things about decorating with secondhand items is giving them new purposes or a fresh face that's just right for your home. The possibilities for adding your own personal stamp to vintage relics are endless. For clever ideas, check out the projects chapter in the back of this book.

ready, set, go
PLAN YOUR OUTING

A little preparation helps ensure a successful day!

Before hitting a flea market, make a wish list of items to look for, including a reasonable value so you don't overpay. It's easy to get caught in the moment, so set a budget and stick to it. Take measurements of your spaces to know what size furnishings and accessories will work. Measure car trunk space, so you don't buy something too large to haul home. Hit the market's website for a list of vendors and their locations. If there is a map, print it and take it with you. Knowing where to find food, restrooms, and delivery services can be a real time-saver. Know the hours and if you can get in early by paying a fee. Be sure to check the forecast and dress comfortably and in layers.

WHAT TO BRING

- Water and a snack
- Hat, sunglasses, sunscreen, bug spray, and an umbrella
- Phone (preferably a smartphone for taking notes and photos) and a charger
- Pen and paper
- Your wish list, measurements, and a map of the market
- Cash and a credit or debit card
- A pull cart, large tote or backpack, and a zippered apron or waist pack to keep hands free
- A magnet to help identify various metals
- Hand wipes and hand sanitizer
- Packing items such as boxes, paper, bubble wrap, plastic stretch wrap, blankets, bungee cords, or rope
- A vehicle to haul your load home

Know the Lingo

As you dabble in the world of all-things-old, it helps to speak the language. Here are a few good terms to know as you shop.

ANTIQUE an item that is 100 years old or older

DICKERING OR HAGGLING negotiating a price

EPHEMERA items, often made of paper, that were not meant to last or hold value

FIRM a price is set and not negotiable

KITSCHY could be considered of poor taste, but appreciated in an ironic way

NEW OLD STOCK items manufactured long ago but never used

PATINA the appearance of an item's surface or finish produced by age, weathering, or use

PRIMITIVES antiques that were handmade, simply designed, and utilitarian

REPRO OR REPRODUCTION a copy made to look like an original

RETRO a style reminiscent of an earlier time period

SMALLS old items that are small

TCHOTCHKE OR KNICKKNACK small decorative items or trinkets not particularly functional

VINTAGE used loosely to describe things of the past, but it technically means belonging to a particular time or era in which an item was made or in fashion

MAKING THE DEAL It's a great feeling to find that perfect treasure, and even better to score an amazing deal. If the price of an item is more than you want to spend, negotiate nicely. Smile and strike up a conversation with the vendor, then ask, "Is this your best price?" Or "Is there any wiggle room in the price?" Offering to pay cash or buying several items can sometimes result in a discount. If you can't settle on a price, ask for a business card or make a note to swing back later in the day or at the very end of the market when the vendor might reconsider the price if it hasn't sold yet. It's OK to walk away empty-handed. You might not make a purchase at every market.

thrill of the hunt

SHOP FLEAS LIKE A PRO

Hone your approach to covering flea markets and buying at secondhand stores. These eight strategies are a good start. Experiment to find what works best for you, then put on your walking shoes, go forth, and conquer.

1

DO A QUICK WALK-THROUGH

Arrive early and scan the entire market quickly, taking notes before slowing the pace to absorb everything. This is the time to snatch up that unbelievable bargain or special treasure you know will sell before you come back.

2

TAKE A GOOD HARD LOOK, THEN DO IT AGAIN

Look a booth over several times because your eye won't register everything the first time. Look up high and down low, not just at eye level. And don't hesitate to dig through boxes or piles.

3

MAKE CONNECTIONS

Become a frequent shopper, hitting a market every time it's held. Get to know the vendors by name and exchange phone numbers. Establishing a relationship might make it easier to strike a deal, and if you let them know what you're looking for, they may call when they have it in stock.

4

IT DOESN'T HURT TO ASK

If you're looking for something specific or are just curious whether a vendor has items not yet set out, don't be afraid to ask. Or if you see a flea-goer carrying something you love, ask where it was purchased.

5
WILL YOU HOLD, PLEASE?

Most vendors will hold your purchases if you ask. That way you don't have to lug them around as you continue to shop. Just remember to pick up your loot before you leave!

7
SIZING THINGS UP

Look for quality craftsmanship and condition, but learn to love imperfections because they go with the territory. Decide whether you can fix an item or live with it as is. If not, move on. Damaged veneer, wobbly furniture legs, and significant cracks in wood or pottery are usually deal-breakers.

8
IDEAS TO STEAL

Some vendors style their booths or shops like professional decorators, creating little showrooms bursting with ideas. Be on the lookout for display and decorating ideas or unique ways to repurpose items. Make notes or take photos if the vendor says it's OK.

6
GO OFF THE BEATEN PATH

Hit small shops and markets that might be less well-known or publicized. Don't pass by a place because it looks rundown—lower overhead costs could mean bargains aplenty await you inside.

cleanup time

SPICK AND SPAN

Freshen up flea market finds to get them ready for home.

Even if you're hesitant to touch that oh-so perfect patina, every secondhand purchase needs a basic cleaning. At the very least remove dust and dirt with a dry or damp rag or a vacuum. Some items might require a bit of elbow grease to clean or refinish surfaces. Here are a few favorite products to have in your cleaning kit. Always research the best way to clean—and to not clean—specific surfaces.

◆ Baking soda

◆ Bar Keepers Friend

◆ Bestine Solvent and Thinner

◆ Disposable nitrile gloves

◆ Disposable shop towels

◆ Goo Gone Spray Gel

◆ Gorilla Wood Glue

◆ Howard Feed-N-Wax Wood Polish & Conditioner

◆ Kramer's Best Antique Improver

◆ Krud Kutter Cleaner/Degreaser

◆ Mr. Clean Magic Eraser

◆ Saddle soap

◆ Scrub brush

◆ White vinegar

COLLECTING

Collecting makes flea outings even more fun! If you've got the itch to start or add to a collection, think about where and how you'll display the items so you look for the right size, color, and style to fit your space. Select a collectible or theme that interests you or has special meaning to you and works into your interior design. You'll want to research the item: Know the item's history, determine how to identify authentic pieces and reproductions, decide what you can expect or are willing to pay, and learn how to care for it. Rare or highly sought-after items fetch higher prices so budget accordingly. But remember, just because something is old doesn't mean it's valuable. There are countless items to collect that won't break the bank, but always buy items in the best condition you can afford. Inventory each item, noting the date and location purchased and the price paid. Be thoughtful and deliberate when arranging collections. Using collections to just fill space can create clutter. Find interesting ways to display like items (grouping them is a must) and rearrange as you add new pieces. Play with height, using books or other objects as risers.

METAL OBSESSION

From farm primitives to factory finds, industrial goods are easy to spy and tempting to try. Bring a little metal home and you'll be hooked.

STEEL Industrial items are often constructed of types of steel, such as galvanized steel or a steel base coated with enamel or porcelain. Look for factory carts and bins, toolboxes, livestock feeders, signs, and more. Steel attracts magnets, so have one handy to test surfaces.

TINPLATE Thin sheets of iron or steel coated with tin are called *tinplate* (which also attracts magnets). Tinplate was commonly used for food containers, decorative ceiling tiles, signs, and toys.

ALUMINUM Stainless steel, copper, brass, and aluminum do not attract magnets. Radiator grills, suitcases, dessert molds, and other kitchenware are a few of the aluminum items you might score.

Color love!

A little rust is OK.

Perfect patina

Unique storage

Attracts magnets

FINE
CRACKERS

Flea Finder

15 FAB U.S. FLEA MARKETS

Expand your horizons. Consider visiting these top venues across the country.

1. THE FARM CHICKS ANTIQUES SHOW

SPOKANE, WA
thefarmchicks.com

2. ROSE BOWL FLEA MARKET

PASADENA, CA
rgcshows.com

3. THIEVES MARKET

TEMPE, AZ
thievesmarketvintageflea.com

4. MILE HIGH FLEA MARKET

HENDERSON, CO
milehighfleamarket.com

5. ROUND TOP ANTIQUES FAIR

ROUND TOP, TX, AND SURROUNDING AREAS
roundtoptexasantiques.com

6. ORONOCO GOLD RUSH DAYS

ORONOCO, MN
goldrushmn.com

7. WHAT CHEER FLEA MARKET

WHAT CHEER, IA
whatcheerfleamarket.com

8. SHIPSHEWANA AUCTION AND FLEA MARKET

SHIPSHEWANA, IN
*shipshewanatradingplace
.com*

9. SPRINGFIELD ANTIQUE SHOW & FLEA MARKET

SPRINGFIELD, OH
springfieldantiqueshow.com

10. NASHVILLE FLEA MARKET

NASHVILLE, TN
nashvilleflea.com

11. SCOTT ANTIQUE MARKETS

ATLANTA, GA
scottantiquemarket.com

12. RENNINGERS ANTIQUE CENTER

MOUNT DORA, FL
renningers.net

13. ANTIQUE EXTRAVAGANZA

ADAMSTOWN, PA, AND SURROUNDING AREAS
antiquescapital.com

14. BROOKLYN FLEA

BROOKLYN, NY
brooklynflea.com

15. BRIMFIELD ANTIQUE AND COLLECTIBLES SHOW

BRIMFIELD, MA
brimfieldshow.com

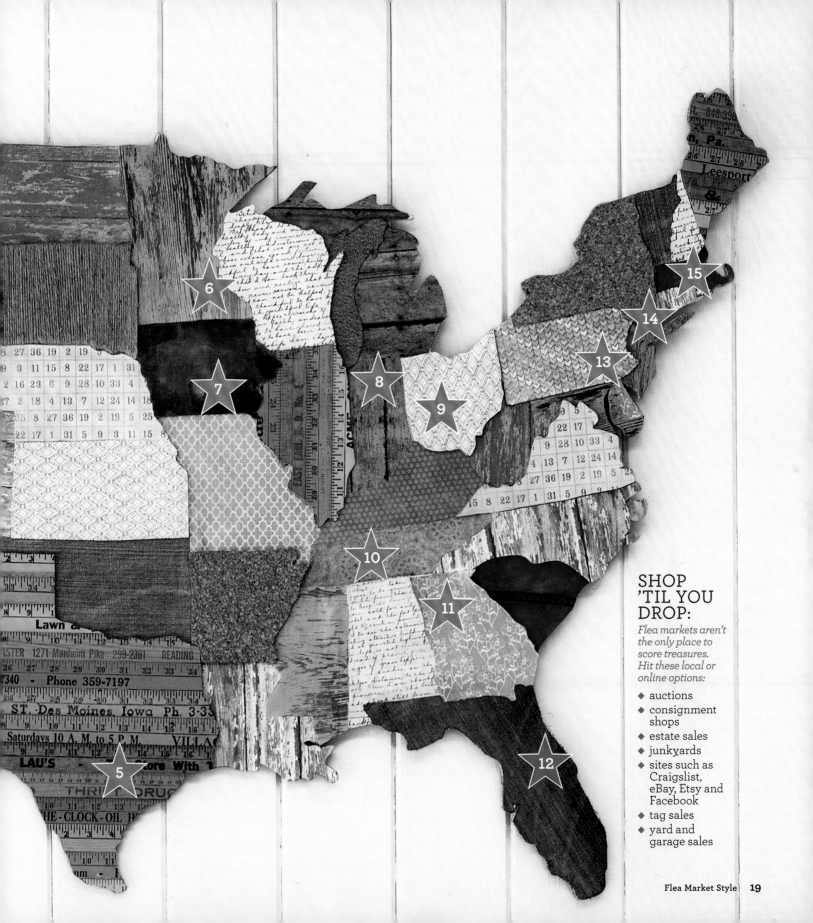

SHOP 'TIL YOU DROP:

Flea markets aren't the only place to score treasures. Hit these local or online options:

- ◆ auctions
- ◆ consignment shops
- ◆ estate sales
- ◆ junkyards
- ◆ sites such as Craigslist, eBay, Etsy and Facebook
- ◆ tag sales
- ◆ yard and garage sales

BOHEMIAN

HOMES

Bold combinations of color and pattern give
boho style its whimsical reputation. Often layered
with a menagerie of eclectic and global treasures,
it embraces pieces with as much personality
as the people who bring them home.

Picture PERFECT

What do you get when a stylist and a photographer pair up?
A one-of-a-kind home that's filled with camera-ready vignettes.

OPPOSITES ATTRACT In the living room, homeowner Caroline Brewer works her styling magic to blend modern and vintage elements, *this photo*. "It's a fun juxtaposition of old and new," she says. A $5 art bargain from a garage sale, *opposite*, holds its own alongside a bold patent leather chair from France.

A walk through Clark and Caroline Brewer's 1920s Nashville bungalow is, for them, like taking a stroll down memory lane. "I started shopping at flea markets and antiques stores because I didn't want my house to feel like everybody else's," Caroline says. "Whenever I travel, I always go to a local flea market. And Clark and I shop together at estate sales or when we're on a trip, so most everything in our home has some type of significance," she says.

The creative couple spends their days designing and documenting beautiful things. Caroline is a stylist for magazines and events and a merchandiser for retail stores. Clark is a lifestyle, travel, and wedding photographer. So when it comes to shopping for their own home, they do so with visually discerning eyes. "My favorites are things that feel clean and modern," Caroline says. "I'm a fan of midcentury pieces. And I can never say no to artwork—especially portraits!"

One thing you won't find at the Brewers' is a large collection of any one item, because Caroline believes the key to an interesting house is in its mix and the composition of unique elements. "I'm drawn to vintage pieces because I have a love of the past and a love of my grandmother's things, but I don't want my home to feel like a dusty antiques store," she says. "Modern elements keep it feeling fresh." The unusual pairing of an old industrial metal chair and a contemporary acrylic table in the living room, for example, speaks to Caroline's fearless approach to combining seemingly disparate styles and textures.

Trusting her gut is one of the things Caroline has learned from her job. When she's shopping, she doesn't get hung up on where something will go or if it will work with things she already has at home. Her mantra is simple: Stay true to what you love, and it will all work together. "I've found that if I go in and try to be specific about what I'm shopping for, the result looks too matchy-matchy," she says.

Another trick of the trade is that nothing should be permanent. Caroline's vignettes evolve with the seasons and with her and Clark's constantly changing tastes. "It's fun to weed out the things we don't both love and then collect new things together that have real meaning," Caroline says. "Each item tells a story."

ARTWORK AND ARTIFACTS Caroline always tries to include a conversation starter in her groupings. A quirky set of children's bowling pins, *above left,* found for $25 on a road trip, fills the role in this little corner. A Tuscan scene from a street artist in Italy floats in a peeling frame above the sleek desk, and the metal chair offers an industrial touch. An eclectic gallery wall in the Brewers' breakfast room, *left,* showcases the couple's passion for collecting art. Caroline either skips a frame or uses new frames that coordinate in color or style to unite photos, ephemera, and paintings.

OLD SCHOOL CHARM Found on a country road, Caroline knew this chalkboard was just the right color and scale to anchor the dining room, *this photo,* and showcase a family crest she had designed and drawn on its humble surface. The primitive farm table was discovered and promptly purchased on a road trip to Louisiana.

BRIGHT IDEA

Add flea market shopping to your agenda when traveling.

Talk to friends and research thrift shops, antiques fairs, and flea markets before you visit a new city. Every place has a different flair, so you never know what you'll find to add to your spaces.

EASY ENTERTAINING
A vintage ironing board, *above left,* serves as an impromptu buffet when entertaining and conveniently folds away when not in use. Etched glasses top plain ones any day. If you can't find a complete set, mix and match vintage glassware for original, easygoing style.

MAPPING IT OUT
To add subtle interest in the hallway, *left,* Clark Brewer stenciled the walls with a modern motif using inexpensive metallic paint. The large pre–World War II map was a fun antiques store find; the pull down-style map likely once hung in a schoolroom.

CARRYING THE LOAD
Even the laundry room, *above,* has its vintage touches. Floral flea market prints adorn the walls next to a retro refrigerator. At just $40, the appliance was quite a bargain, until the couple had to haul it home from an estate sale. "It was so heavy," Caroline says, "it took four of us to move it!"

WORK LIKE A CHARM Caroline and Clark share an upper-level studio space, *this photo,* but the rusty, crusty metal desk—a $5 flea market find—is all Caroline's. An old wood produce crate turned on end makes a perfect display for all of her pretty little things.

MAKE A STATEMENT Layered with playful pillows and linens, the ornate iron guest bed, *this photo,* was a gift from Clark's mother. A metal file cabinet sits bedside along with a retro-style accordion-arm light. The reproduction light plays the part without retrofitting electrical parts into a true vintage model.

MIX MASTER
A quirky papier-mâché deer head, an industrial metal cage pendant light, and a marquee sign letter, *left,* offset Caroline's sweet slipcovered settee. After years in storage, the petite fabric-covered coffee table finally found its place, adding color and personality to this little corner upstairs.

A COMBINED EFFORT
Thanks to a new glass top, a painted cart, *below left,* from an old Nashville laundromat provides display space for Caroline and Clark's curated finds. Because they share a love for decorating , the couple wants the objects and furnishings in their home to truly reflect both of their styles.

NOSTALGIA AT PLAY
During a stay at Brooklyn's Wythe Hotel years ago, the Brewers adored the timeless toile wallpaper in their room so much that they ordered it for their own bedroom, *below.* "I lived in Brooklyn for a summer, so I love that I could incorporate that element," Caroline says.

Renewed PURPOSE

An interior designer rotates
her collections of secondhand
finds seasonally to keep her
traditional North Carolina
space fresh and personal.

FUN AND INFORMAL
Interior designer Lynn-Anne Bruns, *opposite bottom,* collects, among other things, colorful vintage kitchen wares and loves to incorporate her children's crafts when decorating spaces. In her kitchen, *opposite top,* open shelving showcases her collections of pottery and vintage cookbooks as well as a favorite blue enamel coffeepot that cost $10 at an estate sale. The chemistry lab stools came from a thrift store in San Luis Obispo, California, where Lynn-Anne and her family once lived. "They cost us all of $35 each—$10 apiece and $25 for the paint job," she says.

KICK IT UP A NOTCH
Lynn-Anne introduced whimsical color to the screen porch of her 1960s home by wrapping individual boards with wallpaper, *this photo.* The footstool is a tree stump she painted and put on casters.

B rought up on jumble sales in her native Scotland, interior designer and mom of four (six if you count the two dogs) Lynn-Anne Bruns enjoys filling the traditional North Carolina home that she shares with her husband, Ken, with inventive and varied collections. But the amazing part is that it doesn't feel stuffed. The key, Lynn-Anne says, is using a few pieces at a time and rotating collections with the seasons to create fresh new looks. "My home is outwardly exuberant but inwardly calm," she says. "It's a mix of carefully curated objects that are meaningful, fun, and useful."

Everyone in the Bruns house is a collector, but Lynn-Anne is careful about where things appear and what is paired with what. "Every room design is easy to take back to basics and rework depending on the season, event, or whim," she says. Lynn-Anne decorates her home and those of her clients with an eye for backstory and family relevance. She showcases children's toys in glass jars on bookshelves, on mantels, and in bedrooms. She displays old tomes on shelves lined with fabrics that change with the seasons. And she frequently raids attics for retired pieces to create new vignettes—think an heirloom desk placed into service as a hall table.

"It's important for me to find originality and depth in decorating," she says. "If you look carefully at estate sales and flea markets, you'll see objects that mean something to you, that reinforce your sense of self, or reflect what your family's all about." Pieces that make a personal connection are the ones she doesn't hesitate to snatch up.

Estate sales are Lynn-Anne's go-to source for schoolbooks, maps, furniture, and paintings. She frequents country auctions to uncover interesting pieces. "I take the fish-out-of-water approach," she says. "There's just a ton of beautiful and lovingly used things available out in the world that can bring interest and fun to any interior."

Lynn-Anne's kitchen, for example, features a rotating cast of old utensils—wood ones with obvious wear are the most prized. Shelves hold vintage glass bowls, cake plates, and various dessert dishes. "Sometimes I don't even realize I'm collecting until I'm editing and organizing," Lynn-Anne says. "I sometimes collect not by identifiable 'thingness,' but by color or material, or a particular tone or feel. There's a place for new things, but the old things are the best, really."

DECORATE IN LAYERS Lynn-Anne describes her living room, *above left,* as "flea market polished." New upholstered furniture provides a modern foundation for layers of vintage finds, such as mirrors and consignment-store chairs. A playful carved mirror frame, copper candelabras, and a chunky wood table ground the breakfast room, *left,* in rustic fashion, allowing Lynn-Anne to play with color on a set of acrylic chairs. A sampling of her glass jar collection marches down the center of the table. Purchased for $2 to $50, she uses glass jars as vases, luminaries, and containers for holding collections and supplies throughout the house.

EVERY TRICK IN THE BOOK
The den, *this photo,* is filled with refashioned pieces. The sofa was updated with black paint and new upholstery. The table is topped with a piece of acrylic to allow family photos to slide beneath. And the wall of books makes a statement all its own.

Staying Young at Heart

Though rooted in all things old, flea market style needn't make you feel over-the-hill.

CHANGE IT UP Keep spaces fresh and dynamic by changing the scenery seasonally and for the holidays. Swap accessories, rearrange furniture, even paint or wallpaper an accent wall. Seeing spaces in a new way and keeping an open mind can perk you up.

BE NOSTALGIC Collect and display your childhood toys or your children's old toys. Fill vintage jars with plastic animals or toy cars, prop larger toys on shelves, and stack old board games. The memories these hold will fill you with joy.

CATER TO KIDS Decorating with children's handmade arts and crafts. Take kids to the flea market to see what they find. They may see potential in something you don't.

TIME TO PLAY
The decorating scheme for daughter Caroline's bedroom started with a consignment shop patchwork quilt, *far left,* that's more than 70 years old. A polar bear oilcloth print stapled to the wall, an origami mobile, and a hanging sling chair help to complete the fanciful scene.

INDUSTRIAL CHIC
An aged 1930s metal cabinet, *left,* from a hardware store functions as Caroline's bedside table. Multiple-drawer cabinets are rare, and Lynn-Anne snaps them up for clients whenever she can. She often treats them to a fresh coat of paint, but she loved the patina as-is on this one.

A HUB FOR HIM
Maritime maps of Scotland cover the walls in son Alec's room, *above,* highlighting the muted greens of his soda bottle collection. The exit sign and film projector are flea market finds that fit the room's vintage vibe. An old red barrel repurposed as a laundry basket makes chores a little more fun.

Collected WORKS

Curated scores gathered over the years
and hands-on projects layer an Ohio home
in an exuberant sense of style.

TURN THE TABLE
Jennifer (Jen) Harrison, *opposite left,* takes full advantage of her home's wraparound porch, outfitting it with multiple seating areas—complete with rugs and accessories. The $20 carved screen, shell hangings, and settee frame, *opposite right,* are vintage finds. Jen used upholstery cording to weave the back and sides of the settee. Jen's breakfast table, *this photo,* came from a flower shop that was going out of business. It had a great patina, but was too tall, so she cut a foot off each leg.

W hether it's thrifting, fleaing, curbing, or garbage picking, Jennifer Harrison—Jen to her friends and Instagram followers—has done it all in the name of style. She comes by it honestly. "My mom would go garage sale-ing every single weekend," Jen says. "No fail. Thursday, Friday, Saturday, Sunday. Every. Single. Week." Jen was her faithful shadow. Today, Jen and her sister are carrying on the bargain-hunting tradition, even sleeping in their truck on their travels.

Growing up with a carpenter dad, Jen isn't one bit afraid of do-it-yourself projects, and frequently puts her own touch on the treasures she finds. In fact, some would say she's a project machine, modifying and repurposing items to fit into the Cleveland-area home she and her husband, Raymond Ciacchi, built over a decade ago. "I have a very patient husband who allows me to do these crazy experiments," she says.

And experiment she does! Rooms in her house overflow with found furnishings, accessories, rugs, and art that are constantly in flux as she changes things up with the seasons or just because. "I gravitate to relaxed, comfortable, curated, meaningful design," she says. One of Jen's favorite ways to add meaning and depth to a room is with Moroccan textiles. She incorporates them generously throughout her home, connecting spaces with bold color, pattern, and a bit of ethnicity. "I like to create texture and layers, and I'm not afraid to mix things that I love," she says.

What Jen loves has changed a good bit over time. "I started very midcentury modern, then I continued to transition, just like you update and change a wardrobe," she says. "I went eclectic, then French, and fell for antiques. And then a mixture of everything. Then I cleaned all that out and started to go white and simple." While the basis of her look is bohemian and midcentury, she's not a slave to one particular era.

White walls now put Jen's current pared-down finds in the limelight. "I don't collect brands or specific things," she says. "I buy whatever is appealing to my eye at that time." That shopping strategy has paid dividends—Jen's basement storage has style all its own while pieces await their turn upstairs. Thanks to Jen's ability to let go and embrace new favorite things, her home remains fresh and fashionable. "That's the beauty of fleaing and making it myself," she says. "It is affordable to move on to the next thing."

TAKE IT OUTSIDE A 10-foot-long barnwood table, *above left*, invites guests to gab sessions on the porch. "It was built out of barn siding by a gentleman who used to sell farm goods at a market," Jen says. To create romantic garden lighting, Jen uses contractor string from a hardware store to tie candle tapers to bamboo garden sticks, *left*. A rattan peacock chair pairs with midcentury Russell Woodard chairs. Jen scored the metal chairs on Etsy and spray-painted them a sassy pink hue. Now they migrate from space to space whenever extra seating is needed.

WHAT'S IN STORE?
A collection of modern art floats above an antique storefront counter in the living room. "I found the cabinet on Craigslist for $150," Jen says. "The guy had two of them, and he'd already stripped them; I wish I had bought them both!" She originally envisioned it as a kitchen island with a piece of marble on top, but decided to place it hearthside instead.

Make a World of Difference

Moroccan textiles play a big role in Jen Harrison's bohemian-infused home.

RUGS You'll find Moroccan rugs underfoot all over Jen's house. Though many were made to be blankets, she uses them to ground furniture and add vibrant color, pattern, and depth to a room.

PILLOWS AND THROWS Jen strives to make her spaces warm and inviting. "Pillows and textiles do that!" she says. She finds most of her Moroccan treasures on Etsy, eBay, and Instagram from $80 to $350. Quality is important, but age determines the price—older ones can fetch thousands.

BEDDING The cover on the master bed is a Moroccan wedding quilt. Jen admires the workmanship and history of Moroccan pieces and admits they've become a bit of an addiction. "Each one is a piece of art and will never be duplicated," she says.

WHITES AND BRIGHTS Jen's desk, *far left,* is one of her favorite finds, but when she spotted it, she wasn't instantly sure. "I stared at it for 45 minutes and the seller came down $150 while I was deciding," she says. The red chaise, colorful rug, and vintage relics lend more personality to the home office.

THE ULTIMATE PERCH A midcentury daybed from Craigslist nestles nicely into a window niche in the dining room, *left.* Jen plumps the seat with eclectic pillows and a throw. She discovered Moroccan textiles while browsing Pinterest and now has a vibrant collection showcased throughout her house.

PLAYFUL PATTERN When Jen spied the round dining table, *above,* at a local store, she fell in love. She paired it with four bamboo stools she scored for $20 each. Most of the walls in her home are painted white, but here Jen flipped the scheme— dressing walls in bold wallpaper and coating the floor glossy white.

ALONG FOR THE RIDE

Mounted above one of Jen's guest beds, the large horse artwork, *below,* is the focal point of the room. The piece is actually a painted rug she found already framed at a flea market. "It is such an impactful piece, and it makes a statement all by itself!" Jen says. "And it's so ugly, it's great!"

SAFETY IN NUMBERS

Several of the 40-plus paint-by-number pieces Jen collected for a few bucks each at the Springfield Antique Show & Flea Market in Ohio are on display in a guest room, *right.* Jen fashioned the quirky bird pillow out of a chenille bedspread she bought from Goodwill.

FRESH FROM THE FARM

For years Jen had admired an old barn door used as a display piece in a local shop, so when the store closed, she jumped at the chance to buy it. "It was filthy and loaded with pink paint," she says. She rehabbed the piece to create the perfect headboard for the master bedroom, *below right.*

FASHION STATEMENT
In the master bedroom, *this photo,* metal brackets that were once porch railings now support tempered glass to form a vanity. An old dress form and dresser drawers display Jen's collection of vintage and vintage-inspired jewelry and accessories.

COLLECTIONS

1

ANTIQUE BUTTONS

"They're such beautiful little pieces of artwork," Jocie Sinauer says of the thousands of buttons she's collected. She keeps them orderly by organizing them by material—shell, black glass, picture buttons—and by subject matter, such as buttons with birds or plants. Prices vary from a few cents to a few hundred dollars for a rare button. Her favorites are hand-carved mother-of-pearl buttons from the 1780s.

2

GLASS BOTTLES + VASES

Glassware is a versatile and often inexpensive item to collect. Bottles and vases come in many shapes, sizes, and colors and can have fascinating histories. First and foremost, look for pieces with no cracks or chips. Then select what appeals to you. Consider limiting your collecting to a certain color like this sea-glass hue, which is easy to find and less expensive than colors such as cobalt and purple, which are more rare.

3

COSTUME JEWELRY

Originally thought to be knockoffs of the jewels dripping off 1930s screen stars, costume jewelry is having a moment in the spotlight. The jewels' golden age, 1920–1950, saw such designers as Coco Chanel and Christian Dior playing with colorful metal, rhinestones, and beads. Affordable and abundant, costume jewelry looks beautiful piled in a compote or displayed in a pretty frame.

4

ARTWORK

The secret to a great art collection is variety—don't be afraid to mix and match. Contrast modern with vintage or abstract with landscapes, and walls will quickly come to life with personality. Flea markets, estate sales, and even pawn shops can produce art worth "oohing" and "aahing" about at prices any budget can afford. To change the look of an inexpensive piece, hang it in a rich-looking frame or ditch the frame all together.

5

BIRD PRINTS

Mary Schuck has a creative way of gathering art: She simply rips illustrations from old, tattered books. A $10 book handed her 40 vintage bird prints that form a giant grid on her living room wall. She keeps the look casual by setting the pages behind plexiglass. "I'm not a big fan of frames," she says. "I like artwork simple."

6

TOY NODDERS

Also known as bobbleheads or wobblers, *nodders* are spring-loaded papier-mâché figures that rose to popularity in the 1950s. Eventually they were made of ceramic then plastic, and came in the form of everything from sports stars to cartoon characters. Vintage ones like these hula girls add a bit of kitsch to a dresser or shadowbox.

7

ANTLERS

Antlers are made of bone and are commonly shed annually. Before searching parks or other locations, be aware of laws in your area and avoid disrupting wintering animals. If you prefer scouring flea markets to woodland floors, expect to pay $10 to $30, depending on the size and condition. Large quantities typically cost about $10 per pound.

8

BOWLING PINS

Scuffed-up bowling pins are striking a chord with collectors. Pins liberated from the lanes in recent decades are easy to come by and tend to have more graphic appeal than older all-wood models. Brunswick pins, with their signature red crowns are easy-on-the-budget collectibles. Score them for $10 to $75 apiece, depending on the decade and condition.

9

PICTURE FRAMES

"Frames really matter," says New York dealer John Gould. "They make a more dramatic difference than you can imagine." The gleaming finishes of these gilt frames add splendid flair to walls. Budget-conscious shoppers might grab a plain wood frame and a can of metallic gold spray paint in lieu of a true gilt frame.

BOHEMIAN

10

COPPER JEWELRY

Debuting in the 1930s, copper jewelry hit its heyday in the 1950s and is having a resurgence today as it easily mixes with casual, blue-jean lifestyles. From Native American to high-designer pieces, there is a wide range of prices, which makes building a large collection doable without a big investment.

11

WHIMSICAL CARVINGS

These intricate wood carvings are fashioned by self-taught artists, making them fine examples of American outsider folk art. Examine each piece to appreciate the craft and creativity. You might happen across a $20 bargain, but highly unusual, elaborate carvings can go for hundreds. Display them with a little elbowroom so they get noticed.

12

POLITICAL BUTTONS

A time-honored tradition in American politics, campaign buttons make a colorful collectible. The first political buttons were made for the 1896 presidential race between William McKinley and William Jennings Bryan. Common buttons, such as the 1972 "Nixon Now" button, can be found for a dollar, while rare buttons from the '20s might be worth thousands.

13

BRASS OBJECTS

Brass is back and it's capturing a new generation of followers at flea markets. "Vintage brass lends a trendy touch of metallic to a space without being too bold or overpowering," says collector Amy Wilens, who sells curated brass pieces. Because antique brass can be heavy, expensive, and overwhelming to a room, Wilens suggests seeking smaller pieces such as candlesticks and animal figurines.

14

STATE PLATES

Souvenir plates, which date to the 1870s, became popular when travel became more accessible. Keep your eyes open for big-name manufacturers such as Vernon Kilns and Homer Laughlin. Find signed or unsigned plates at flea markets or online for $5 to $35.

COTTAGE
HOMES

Inviting and personal, cottage style is all about being casual and carefree. Fresh beachy blues, vintage greens, and sweet pinks mingle with pretty patterns to create oh-so charming spaces.

Worth The
JOURNEY

Stripped to the studs, this
1940s Nashville cottage now
reflects its owner's abiding
passion for treasure hunting.

FINDING COMMON GROUND
Exposed brick contrasts with pristine white siding, *opposite top,* on the reinvented cottage Amy Jacobs shares with her goldendoodles, Patsy Cline and June Carter. She displays favorite travel-theme treasures, including antique maps and globes on the fireplace ledge, *opposite bottom.* As part of her sightseeing motif, Amy hung large-scale depictions of the White House and the United States on her living room wall, *this photo.*

W hy do you fall in love with a house? For Amy Jacobs, the decision to purchase this 1940s cottage in Nashville's 12th South neighborhood was always about the journey of making it her own. That vision helped her see through the dilapidated disarray of water-damaged walls and buckled flooring. It empowered her to strip the dilapidated materials down to the studs and start over. "My sister thought I was crazy," Amy recalls. But with the help of a contractor, walls were removed and doorways added to open up the space. The roof was even torn off to form a master suite complete with repurposed rafters.

Amy tried to give each room or space something special, whether reclaimed flooring, salvaged windows, or a custom door. The result is a jewel box of a home with unique architectural moments that charm and surprise at every turn.

After nailing down her renovation choices, Amy set about furnishing her cottage with years of meaningful items acquired while scavenging for vintage treasures. "I don't shop at just one vendor—I like to hunt and gather for all the right pieces," she says of her methodology. She scoured flea markets, thrift stores, and websites for items that spoke to her love of rustic nature and travel.

Expanses of crisp white paint and tile balanced by richly stained floors create a versatile backdrop for Amy's cherished collections. High, open walnut shelves in her streamlined kitchen serve as a showcase for framed farm animal prints that match the room's rough-hewn aesthetic. The cottage's fireplace mantel is home to travel-themed art and antique gems. She arranges and rearranges framed prints, adding excursion-related quotes, maps, globes, and even miniature suitcases.

From graphic accent pillows coordinated throughout the cottage to industrial kitchen table legs found on a farm, every decoration and piece of furniture fits Amy's effort to create a lived-in retreat. "More than anything, I want to create a home that sets people at ease—a place that feels like their home, too."

DOOR TO DOOR
Flanked by custom-made double doors, *opposite,* the living room fireplace hosts a revolving collection of art prints and antiques store finds. The Dutch door is open as much as the weather allows—friends and neighbors drop by often.

A STEP UP A salvaged door in its original distressed state, *far left,* glides along barn door hardware, opening to reveal a gray-and-white-painted stairway that climbs to Amy's favorite space—the master suite. Mounted on clipboards, an ever-changing collection of typography and old photos brings the wall to life.

CENTER OF ATTENTION
Crafted from linen napkins sewn end to end, the dining room's table runner, *above left,* grounds a centerpiece composed of an old metal tool tray, canning jars, and blooms of golden ranuncula.

SOPHISTICATED TOUCH Soothing gray walls in the dining room, *left,* enjoy shots of personality with traditional-style embroidered draperies and bold red accents. The vintage-style pendant light and ticking stripe rug keep the cottage theme going strong.

Hunting and Pecking

Amy Jacobs uses a variety of techniques to find all the right pieces.

RECYCLE Weave salvaged and recycled materials into a space or use them to construct something new. Amy rescued doors, used reclaimed wood, and incorporated old relics to establish genuine cottage style throughout her home.

REPRO Puritans cringe at the thought of reproduction pieces, but the truth is, they are readily available, affordable, and look more authentic every year. There's no shame in using a few vintage-style pieces, but let your main focus be on the real deal when possible.

RETAIL Sometimes brand spankin' new just makes sense. Take kitchen appliances, light fixtures, or a sofa, for instance. It's a delicate balance, but modern touches can help the old stuff really shine.

CLASSIC CHOICES
Amy splurged on the white apron-front sink and cabinetry, *above,* but then opted for reasonably priced subway tile on the backsplash. Concrete countertops, custom hickory shelving, and dish towel café curtains round out the room.

ON THE LEVEL
Amy composes an art arrangement, *right,* using vintage levels and an interactive chalkboard map that can chart her travels and favorite locations. A red storage bench anchors the grouping and hides table linens and serving pieces in the dining room.

ALL THE FIXIN'S
The renovated kitchen, *far right,* blends the best of modern with rustic charm. Stainless-steel appliances pair nicely with reproduction stools and lighting. Amy found the industrial metal legs for the walnut-topped island in a barn.

Anchors Away

Select one item to anchor or really drive the look of a room.

QUILT LOVE Amy wanted to use the colorful Dresden Plate quilt her grandmother made, so she let it take center stage at the end of her bed and then selected accessories, textiles, and artwork that worked with the handcrafted treasure.

TO THE RESCUE
The master suite, *above,* features ceiling beams salvaged from the original roof rafters. Rather than toss extra wood flooring, Amy had it made into a hardworking storage trunk for the foot of the bed. Colorful flower paintings from a flea market in Europe line the narrow ledge.

DELIGHTFUL REFLECTION
Rather than mount one large mirror in the master bathroom, *right,* Amy displays a collection of round and oval mirrors on the white subway tile wall. She had a media cabinet retrofitted for her sink because the size was perfect for the long, narrow fixture.

BEDSIDE MANNER
Next to the guest bed, *above*, Amy situated a vintage school desk to serve as a bedside table. Above the bed she hung a whimsical raffle wheel. "The floral pillow served as inspiration for the color palette," says Amy, who selected modern bed linens with fresh cottage motifs.

THE BUILDING BLOCKS
The bones of a room help set the tone so Amy made every effort to use period-style architectural elements at every turn. In the guest bathroom, *above right*, window and base moldings, hexagonal tiles, a classic pedestal sink, and wainscot lend cottage style.

SERVING A PURPOSE
Amy repurposed a metal grocery store potato chip display and milk glass compote, *right*, as playful jewelry holders. The petite dining room server was painted green and repurposed as a dressing vanity in the bedroom.

Test of
TIME

This seen-it-all structure in a historic
Rhode Island neighborhood is both
tranquil and lively at the same time.

INTO THE BLUE Wood plank floors and matchstick blinds give the dining room, *this photo,* some weight and keeps the sea-hue room from feeling too frothy. Homeowner Nancy Chace found the chairs at a consignment shop and painted them white. The dining hutch, *opposite,* a $400 score at a local flea market, cradles a medley of inexpensive peacock blue dishes, Mason jars, and pitchers.

At the intersection of function and fun, vintage and new, and work and play sits a century-old cottage belonging to Nancy and Rick Chace, along with daughters Phoebe and Claire. Just a stone's throw from the coast, the house is nestled among shops and restaurants in the historic district of Bristol, Rhode Island. "It's a beautiful and wonderfully walkable waterfront community," Nancy says. "A quintessential New England town—settled in 1680."

The house itself was built in 1896 and has undergone many changes over the decades. Under the Chace family's stewardship, the house was recently refurbished. The renovated kitchen, once tiny and storage-starved, is now blessed with abundant cabinetry, banquette seating, and an adjacent mudroom.

Other rooms have flourished under Nancy's uncanny knack for combining old furnishings with new, punctuating rooms with industrial pieces, and accenting it all with happy hues. The dining room notably gathers elements across eras for a design that transcends time. It features midcentury ladder-back chairs, a 15-year-old farmhouse table, a Victorian Era mantel, a new arched mirror, and gleaming wood floors that date to 1914 (not original to the house but plenty old nonetheless). Each piece received special treatment—whether a wash of paint, smart slipcovers, or a jaunty tablecloth—to come into the fold. And it's all enveloped by a wall color that shifts from blue to green with the sunlight.

A similarly splashy hue—one part Provence and two parts Old White from Annie Sloan's Chalk Paint line—imparts a dreamy glow in the master bedroom. The color was Nancy's starting point for the room, and it sparked every other purchase: vintage spool tables as nightstands, a yard-sale chair, and bedding both new and old. Though the blues and greens don't exactly match each other, "they work happily together," Nancy says. "For me, the colors are soothing because they all harmonize."

"Cottages can be time capsules," Nancy says. New owners often add their own touches to furnishings before passing them on to successive generations. "This cottage is a witness of sorts," she says. "Its belongings and collections take on a unique personality. I relish things with a story." Imparting her story—and carefree style—on this home is perfectly fitting.

ONE-OF-A-KIND A barn red door marks the entrance to Sea Rose Cottage, Nancy's working studio and retail shop that occupies the front rooms of the home, *above left.* Anchoring one end of the dining room, a behemoth storage cabinet, *left,* is from a 19th-century tool factory. A wide vintage sign—one of homeowner Nancy's weaknesses—completes the picture-perfect vignette.

VITAL REVAMP
The formerly cramped kitchen, *far left,* is now a roomy remodeled cook space boasting natural light, creamy white cabinetry, and pops of midcentury color.

CASUAL CORNER
Most Chace family meals happen around this built-in banquette in the kitchen, *left.* The vintage sign was a fortuitous flea market find that Nancy snapped up despite the price. "Ever since we got it, nearly every family photo is around that sign," she says.

THE RIGHT DIRECTION
Antique maps, *right,* depict three Rhode Island towns. Nancy opted to frame them to serve as artwork and color inspiration for the living room. Blues and greens plucked from the maps' rivers and streams perk up the room's neutral color palette.

CAREFREE RETREAT Spindles, caning, and painted surfaces lend old-time flair to furniture in the master bedroom, *this photo,* as does the vintage chenille bedspread. Nancy set her heart on the wall color—a shade of blue chalk-finish paint—and then hunted yard sales and shops for new and old items to match.

KEEPING IN STEP
Once walled off, the stairwell is now bright and open on the main level, *left*. To echo the warm floors, Nancy had the railing and newels stained rather than painted. The stair treads match the blue walls, allowing them to pop against the original white beaded-board wainscoting.

ORDER IN THE HOUSE
Just off the kitchen, the mudroom features the cottagey white-and-green palette as well as a storage cubby for everyone in the house, *below left*. Across from the cubbies resides a drop zone to charge electronics and organize mail, homework, and the busy family calendar.

SERENE SCENE
A beachy seafoam hue sets the stage in the main-level bathroom, *below*. A half-wall allows sunshine to stream into the tub enclosure. A basket, striped bath mat, and seashells add charm and texture alongside period-style floor tiles and light fixtures.

Savor the
MOMENTS

In a house filled with rich history,
renovated spaces meet modern needs
and help a young family stay focused
on the present.

ALL IN THE FAMILY Yasmine McGrane, *opposite left,* credits her Swiss-French mother for passing on her penchant for simple pleasures and passion for a good flea market. An old metal cart off the kitchen, *opposite right,* stands ready to roll wherever it's needed. Slipcovered chairs, woolly throws, and piles of pillows, *this photo,* lend soft surroundings to the custom stainless-steel gas fireplace and cater to relaxed afternoons of reading and family games around the reclaimed-wood factory cart.

Yasmine McGrane savors life like it's a warm bowl of café au lait, each sip a pleasant awakening. Just over 16 years ago, she left a fast-paced dot-com career in search of better balance in her busy life. For the next decade, she happily ran a successful home design store, which she infused with the unhurried spirit of her Montréal childhood.

But after her children, Finnegan and Delphine, were born, Yasmine yearned to rebalance yet again. "I wanted to enjoy the simple moments with them," she says. "A bird singing. The rain falling." That quest has flowered into an ideal she calls "white-space living," in which mindfulness brings pleasure both in life and at home.

To find that white space for herself, Yasmine closed her brick-and-mortar store and moved it online. She planted an organic garden. And she and her husband, David, renovated their 1893 Victorian home to make it more conducive to family living. They relocated the kitchen to larger quarters to foster cooking with their kids and capture uplifting views of San Francisco Bay. They turned their home's generous entry hall into a dining room for hosting unstressed gatherings of friends.

In every room, Yasmine enhances the calm surroundings with vintage treasures—many from the French flea markets she loves—chosen for their ability to energize and spark creativity. And the fact that so many things throughout the house are secondhand finds means the family creates a smaller carbon footprint.

Though they are in the heart of the city, Yasmine and David are determined to live life at a slower pace and have created an environment in which their family can do that. Through their renovation, they retained the original charm and soul of the home while adding modern elements to meet their lifestyle. Their home now lives like a breath of fresh air; yoga, meditation, reading, gardening, and laughing trump office time.

"If your home is aligned with your values, your life flows with it," Yasmine says. Her intention is to be present for what each day offers: eating Popsicles on the porch, engaging in painting sessions after school, walking to the farmers market or along the edge of the water. "We often overlook those ordinary moments," Yasmine says. "But it's those moments that can bring us such peace and joy."

WORTH A THOUSAND WORDS A harvest table, *above left,* in the McGrane home doubles as a studio space for the kids, who paint with abandon on a continuous supply of kraft paper. A milk-bottle caddy from Holland keeps brushes handy at all times. A few salvaged barn doors stand propped against walls in Yasmine's home. Flaunting a weathered painted patina, this barn relic, *left,* hosts a gallery of exuberant—and always changing—artwork.

LONG SHELF LIFE Vintage bowls and kitchenware in cheery colors stand at the ready on open shelving, calling cooks of all ages to action in the updated kitchen, *this photo.* Here modern conveniences share space with thoughtfully collected and placed accessories from years gone by.

A WARM WELCOME Yasmine extended her rejuvenating and easy-living design ideas to the 1910 carriage house, *this photo,* behind the family's home. Found treasures—glass bottles, a lab beaker, an old oil painting, and wood step stool—layer the space, which functions as a guesthouse, with inviting touches.

Give spaces more meaning by letting possessions draw on the past.

Keep vintage treasures around you that bring out your authentic self, whether it's old rolling pins that remind you to bake or a stack of worn suitcases that inspire you to travel.

JUST YOUR TYPE
Guests who stay in the McGranes' carriage house are treated to special quotes tucked in a vintage typewriter, *above.* The do-it-yourself desk was fashioned from a rescued door and a pair of sawhorses painted white.

CONNECT TO NATURE
Vintage tins are aplenty at thrift stores and flea markets. Yasmine reuses her tea tins to make a little herb garden on the windowsill, *above right,* which nudges her to brew a cup of tea and unwind a little.

BY THE NUMBERS
A portion of a worn mainsail hung as a headboard in the master bedroom, *right,* inspires David McGrane to make time for sailing. The pillow at bedside—originally designed as a dog bed—is now Yasmine's spot for daily meditations.

SORT IT OUT Finnegan, an avid reader, corrals his many books in an old French cabinet with numbered cubbies, *below.* Connecting with music is another favorite pastime, as he practices strumming his guitar atop a hand-me-down chair concealed by a patriotic cover.

TIMELESS TREASURES Yasmine shares Earth-friendly learnings with her kids by furnishing their rooms with vintage pieces—which consume no new resources. A collection of heirloom toys and books top Delphine's quaint antique dresser, *right,* evoking the essence of childhood.

IN FINE TUNE Tucked beneath the eaves, *below right,* Finnegan's bed was constructed of reclaimed wood. Vintage toys fill shelves and an antique French table soccer game entices even tech-loving friends to stretch out and play. A porthole-inspired window punctuates the room's sailing theme.

PRETTY PLAYGROUND A posy-covered quilt brightens Delphine's flea market bed, which is graced by a gauzy canopy, *this photo.* Yasmine dresses beds with durable Belgian linens meant to last a lifetime. The blue velvet chair is a vintage find as is the wood bread crate. Both make nice landing pads for Delphine's favorite stuffed animals.

COLLECTIONS

1

BISCUIT TINS

Made from tinplate, biscuit tins were designed to hold cookies or candy. They emerged in England in the 1860s after a law was passed allowing groceries to be sold in individual packaging. As lithographing technology improved, manufacturers were able to print colorful designs directly onto metal. The tins made economic sense, as consumers were willing to spend more for the decorative tin than for the treats inside.

2

BAKELITE UTENSILS

A hard plastic developed in 1907, Bakelite appeared on the handles of flatware and kitchen utensils in the late 1920s, bringing color and personality to the kitchen. Sold for 5 cents in the 1980s, a solid color fork goes for $10 today. Utensils with a checkerboard or polka-dot pattern are more rare and can sell for more than $200. Display in jars, allowing the pretty handles to show. If buying for use, select stainless steel instead of chrome plated.

3

WIRE BASKETS

Sandy Koepke has collected wire baskets for over 35 years, using them to organize linens, makeup, office supplies, and kitchenware. "A lot of them are Early American and from France," she says. "I like them because they're pragmatic; they have multiple uses." Flea markets and antiques shops are Sandy's go-to sources, but she admits vintage ones are getting harder to find. She suggests watching out for reproductions and rust.

4

HAND-PIECED QUILTS

Quiltmaking has been a popular pastime in America since the 1700s, and today quilts are highly collectible as works of folk art with historical significance or as prized family heirlooms. Quilts are typically categorized by pattern such as Rose of Sharon or Grandmother's Flower Garden, and though the materials used in quilts vary widely, cottage collectors are fond of those fashioned from old feed sacks or worn-out clothing.

5

CAKE STANDS

Whether petite or grand, cake stands make a sweet kitchen collectible. Expect to pay anywhere from $2 to $50, depending on size, condition, and character. Fancier ones might fetch more. Look for Depression glass, milk glass, hobnail, and other desired styles. Display them in stacks or use them as risers to give smaller objects a step up to get noticed.

6

SEED DISPLAY BOXES

Before catalogs and garden centers, merchants hawked seeds in wood boxes adorned with vivid garden scenes. "I love the surprise of opening a seed box and seeing the antique lithograph picture with lettering and floral graphics," collector Stephanie Brandenburg says. Popular in the 1800s to 1920s, the boxes are hard to find and can cost hundreds. But you might stumble upon one for less.

7

BOOKS

Old books often have covers worthy of artwork status, with colorful illustrations and embossed patterns that might even carry over to the spine and back cover. Select a topic you love, like these gardening books, and look for copies free of tears or stains.

8

MILK GLASS

Milk glass has been around since the 16th century, but the term, meaning opaque colored glass, wasn't coined until the 20th century when it became popular in American households. Milk glass comes in various colors, but white is a classic cottage staple. Many shapes, patterns, and makers exist, so do your homework before buying.

9

CHALKWARE DOGS

James A. Baggett's 73 kitschy chalkware pups speak to his love of all things canine. Originally carnival prizes in the 1940s and '50s, chalkware figurines are colorful and can be delicate. "The first one I bought was particularly distraught-looking," James says. "It looked like it needed a home." His rule: Never spend more than $10.

COTTAGE

10

SOUVENIR COASTERS

Ceramic travel coasters are the kind of tourist item people love to collect. They're quirky and personal and tell a story of another place and time. These little trivets pull triple duty: artwork, coaster, and conversation starters. When displaying, group them in multiples to get the look of a larger piece of art.

11

TOY VEHICLES

Collecting toys of any kind is pure fun, and in the mid-1800s American makers were making toys from tinplate and cast iron. Later, pressed steel was the material of choice, and when baby boomers came on the scene, they created a huge market for toy autos. Look for models with working components and in good condition.

12

ARTISAN POTTERY

Originally in the business of making bricks, Haeger Potteries transitioned to pottery pieces in 1912. Featuring a special durable glaze, the pottery has evolved and endured over the decades. Collector Susan Ford has paid as little as 50 cents and as much as $40 for a piece and loves treasure hunting for them at thrift shops and estate sales.

13

HANDBLOWN BOTTLES

In production since 1938, handblown water bottles produced by the Blenko Glass Co. are one of the West Virginia-based manufacturer's most successful and enduring products. The bottles come in a variety of vibrant hues, shapely designs, and textures, and vintage ones can often be found starting at $15.

10

11

12

13

14

FISHING BUOYS

These wood relics are a type of float that was attached to a net or trap by fishermen and lobstermen. They would use the uniquely painted, shaped, and marked buoys to easily identify the nets or traps they'd set in the water. Look for buoys that are naturally weathered by years in the water but still flaunt some of the original paint. The going rate is about $30 to $50.

COUNTRY

HOMES

Rustic relics and plenty of patina are badges of honor in country-style homes. Whether you're after a cozy cabin feel or primitive farmhouse look, think rough-hewn woods and furnishings battered by the elements.

Revolving
DESIGN

In a Tennessee farmhouse, rustic and refined unite to produce a sophisticated interior that resonates with timeless charm.

CASUAL GATHERING
Tracy and Tom Smith's
farmhouse presides over
12 acres of land in Franklin,
Tennessee. The side
yard, *opposite,* is home to
a kitchen garden. Tracy
scored a set of 1970s
chairs with French-style
silhouettes for a song and
then stapled vintage burlap
to the seats to foster a
sense of rustic elegance in
the dining room, *this photo.*

The only constant in Tracy and Tom Smith's Tennessee, farmhouse is that rooms are always evolving. The main cast of characters includes beloved furniture from Tracy's mom, a collection of quadruple-plate silver dishware, and a gaggle of chandeliers, but where each item will be on any given day is always a surprise. She's not afraid to move an old carpenter's table or bright blue chair from room to room to see where it might look best. "It's just that I like change, so I try things," Tracy says. "Tom is a dear sport about it. He says that most people come home from work to see what's for dinner. He comes home to see where the couch is!"

Tracy credits her mom, Nancy Eversole Bible, with passing on a love of antiquing, raw wood, and cozy surroundings. Though she's a regular at Preservation Station (a local salvage store) and the Nashville Flea Market, her thrifting exploits aren't limited to the obvious options. Tracy has been known to scope out flea markets while on vacation and to "shop" at her mom's house. "If she came in and said she wanted her things back," Tracy says, "it would be a very empty house!"

When a secondhand treasure doesn't work out as is, Tracy will consider giving the item a new purpose or will roll up her sleeves to revamp it: She added casters to the narrow kitchen table and often re-covers or repaints furnishings to suit her style.

Antique mirrors and architectural salvage are found throughout the house, imparting sassy sparkle and rich character. Old mirrors of all shapes and sizes cluster on the walls, reading as artwork but without all the busyness. "I really like mirrors," Tracy says. "There's a lot of light and a lot of white in this house—I love the reflection of light. The mirrors play off of the more primitive or rustic pieces, lightening their heaviness."

Salvaged windows and doors grace doorways, cabinets, and hutches—they're Tracy's secret defense against lackluster architecture. "You can transform a really boring or plain room with one cool door," she says. "A door can change a room's whole look and add a focal point." Neutral backdrops, such as white walls, simple curtains, and pine floors, give Tracy the freedom to mix things up while allowing her salvaged items to shine. "I keep working on it," Tracy says. "The house is just a work in progress."

VINTAGE VIBRANCE One of Tracy's few concessions to bold, bright color comes in her foyer, *above left*, where riotous wallpaper she snatched up at 75 percent off stands up to a 7-foot-tall salvaged hall mirror and a French chair covered in electric-blue vinyl. Tracy's mom is responsible for starting her collection of quadruple-plate silver, *left*. "Both my mom and I collect this. I love using them for decor, holding silverware or flowers," she says. She finds many pieces at flea markets, antique stores, and on eBay. "I love that it is less formal," she says of the patina. "I don't polish it."

RELAXED ATMOSPHERE
The living room coffee table, *this photo,* came from Tracy's brother's workshop. She flipped the boards to hide an orange wood sealant and replaced the legs with plumbing pipes so the piece would sit at the desired height.

SALVAGE SMART
The kitchen's upper cabinets, *opposite,* are vintage bookcases Tracy flipped and hung on the wall. Reclaimed wood was used to make the base cabinet doors. The table was once an old carpenter's table. "I bought that thing for $100, added the wheels," she says. Use a food-safe sealer on furnishings that may come into contact with food.

DIVINE DISPLAY
Coated with layers of old blue, gray, and cream paint, the Gustavian wedding hutch, *above,* was a gift from Tom and has been in four different rooms over the years.

COZY CORNER In the den, *above right,* architectural relics top one of the many old tables Tracy has collected. The leopard-print chair and pendant light add touches of industrial and chic styles to this country space.

FASHION PLATES
The English dishware, *right,* dates to the late 1800s and was manufactured by George Jones & Sons. "It has a very dainty, happy pattern on it," Tracy says. "And it goes with my green Depression dessert glasses."

TWO OF A KIND

In the small bathroom Tracy's daughters share, *below,* symmetry prevails. The pair of frameless mirrors and petite wall-hung sinks are reproductions, but do the trick to keep things light, bright, and in keeping with the enchanting style of the home.

IN THE ROUGH

For a charming pass-through to the laundry room, Tracy salvaged a diamond-grid window, *right.* She never considered repainting, instead allowing the chippy weathered paint finish to show its age. "You can just tell they're original," she says.

FUN-LOVING SPIRIT

Tracy's 14-year-old daughter, Hanna, gravitates to an eclectic mix of things in her bedroom. One quaint corner, *below right,* showcases an old storage trunk from her grandmother, a tablecloth hung as a curtain, and a hanging disc chair to chill in.

PLAYFUL GETAWAY Hanna has strong opinions about the design of her bedroom. Chalkboard paint and painted planks create a charming backdrop for flea market objects—marquee letter, mirror, and bedside table—and sweet vintage-inspired bedding.

Summertime
DREAMS

Guided by a vision of what
summer camp used to be,
a Chicago couple return a
storied Wisconsin getaway to
rustic glory with thrifty finds.

David Hernandez wants you to carve your initials into his furniture. He'll even lend you a pocketknife if you reach the bunkhouse and realize you have no way to leave your mark. This is summer camp, after all. And at Camp Wandawega, camp rules are the rule. David and his wife, Tereasa Surratt, bought the 25-acre, 80-plus-year-old camp in Wisconsin in 2004 with a plan to renovate a piece of history. After 10 years of work, the camp has emerged as an island of nostalgia that seems equal parts movie set, pop-culture museum, and archaeological site. Tereasa crafted each of the property's spaces as an authentic set piece picturing a moment from the 1920s to the 1960s. And she did it all with a budget of $200 per room.

Treasures unearthed on the property itself helped Tereasa keep costs in check. Those finds account for about one-quarter of the camp's decor, but the other three-quarters came from Tereasa's tireless shopping at flea markets and secondhand sales. Salvaged throwback items, such as varsity letters, wool blankets, needlepoint art, and a variety of vintage sporting equipment, are at the heart of the camp's charm. Their histories call out to David and Tereasa, and they speak to overnight guests who see the appeal in a vacation that requires a hike to the shower house. Consider one of Tereasa's finds: a bin of 50 doilies priced at less than 50 cents each. "How many people do you know that can make a doily?" she says. "They're incredible pieces of art someone's grandmother made."

Preserving ties to the past and keeping the camp spirit alive motivate the couple to remain on the hunt for more cabins to move to the property. And while they call Wandawega a resort, they want potential guests to understand exactly what they're signing up for. "People say, 'It's open air and bugs can get in!'" David says. "Yeah, that's how camping used to be."

SUNNY HUES Yellow chairs in the dining hall, *opposite,* echo a collection of Fiesta dishware discovered behind a false wall in the kitchen. Chalkboard paint transforms cabinets into message boards and an old wall bookrack holds pamphlets outlining various local activities.

THE LODGE LIFE The old bunkhouse, *far left,* once served as a brothel. Today, simple rooms, vintage furnishings, a communal kitchen and parlor, and shared restrooms offer guests a no-frills getaway experience similar to the one David and his family experienced when they visited the camp in the 1970s.

IN WORKING ORDER An existing camp relic, the ancient General Electric fridge, *above left,* still works, "but weighs as much as a truck," Tereasa says. Other items of the era—metal fan, tea towels, and dishware— were picked up at various markets and tag sales.

SELF-SERVICE Wandawega guests get to prepare their own meals in one of four kitchens on the grounds. The main kitchen, *left,* is a thoughtful mix of modern and vintage. "We are really 95 percent vintage at camp,""Tereasa says.

BRIGHT IDEA

Group similar items to create a thoughtful themed display.

Tereasa and David found more than 150 collectibles on the camp property. The pieces looked like junk and clutter until they organized and displayed them by category.

SIT A SPELL On the sunporch, fresh paint and Hudson Bay blanket-covered cushions gave new life to a wicker rocking chair, *above left,* found on the property of Camp Wandawega. Badminton rackets serve as decoration but are also ready for play.

TO THE LETTER Various patches from letterman's sweaters and jackets appear around the camp. In the lodge, Tereasa used an Irish wool sweater from a thrift store to cover the seat of a $15 chair, *left,* and added the H on top. Vintage megaphones she'd had for years now reside at camp.

STATE OF THE ART Situated right off the lake, this cabin, *above,* has nostalgic views inside and out. The wood-slat chair was handed down from a friend, and the wall collage was fashioned from flea and thrift scores Tereasa had been hoarding for years.

CABIN FEVER Most of the bed frames, such as this iron twin, *this photo,* are original to the property. A mix of colorful patterned linens adds vintage personality, and a simple line of lanterns creates an artistic composition against newly exposed rafters. Like most of the rooms, this cabin is painted white to make touch-ups and repainting easier year after year.

AUTHENTIC ARTIFACTS
A thrift store typewriter and writing desk, *above left,* join a wood folding chair (painted campy green to match the room's trim) to capture the nostalgia of a past era. "My rule is it won't cross the threshold if it's newer than the 1960s," Tereasa says.

MAKE ARRANGEMENTS
Put relics to work to create chic artwork and accessories on the cheap. For this avant-garde wall arrangement, *left,* Tereasa hung $3 tag sale arrows in a fun design, then topped it with a mounted fish head—one of many items found at the camp.

A NEW PURPOSE
"We didn't want to pay retail for anything," Tereasa says. An old Girl Scout camp yielded the outhouse-turned-shower building, *above,* where salvaged spigot handles serve as towel hooks inside and an old fishing buoy adorns the outside.

From Trash
to Treasure

*See the value
in castoffs and
unearthed relics.*

TEREASA'S MOTTO:
"It's the memories that
matter, not the price
or pedigree. Freebies
or near-freebies, such
as seashells or themed
vacation souvenirs,
count as collectibles."

TWO-BY-TWO
Signaling flags flank an
old mirror to provide
artwork above the beds
in this cabin, *above.*
Two metal desk lamps
and the dresser were
also secondhand finds.
Arrows in a Thermos
are Tereasa's clever and
everlasting alternative to
fresh flowers in a vase.

SLEEP ON IT
Late 1950s curtains,
left, inspired this guest
room's boyish decor.
Vacation pennants
tacked to a wool blanket
produce a colorful, camp-
classic feel, as does the
kitschy carved totem pole
table lamp.

Innovative VINGAGE

Hand-me-downs, curbside treasures, and
flea market scores—all cleverly repurposed—
bring modern energy and fresh style to a
turn-of-the-century New York home.

AS GOOD AS NEW The living room's sofa, *this photo,* is the only new piece of furniture Leona Beck, *opposite left,* has in her home. She softens its youth by piling on accent pillows crafted from vintage toile and grain sacks. Antique game boards—a collection launched after Leona's mother gifted her a cribbage board—climb the wall above. Metal meat hooks from an old butcher shop, *opposite right,* announce Leona's style at the door. She blunted the tips with a metal file before installing.

O ne. That's the total number of purchased-new furniture items in Leona Beck's entire Saratoga Springs, New York, home. Everything else, including tables, chairs, and even beds, was either found secondhand or fondly passed down from family or friends. "Why buy something new," Leona asks, "when there's already so much great stuff out there with character and charm?"

Indeed. Leona's warm brand of retro-industrial style is courtesy of a long list of storied finds. Each has an interesting tale to tell, and each contributes to the newest chapter in the life of the 1902 Queen Anne–style home Leona shares with her husband, Tom, and their two teenage sons. The home underwent a modernizing rehab after the couple purchased it, renovating a few key spaces like the kitchen and mudroom and redecorating everything else. "We moved into a lot of heavy draperies and wallpaper, but we knew we could make it our own in time," Leona says.

And so they did. Take the oh-so charming bench at the foot of Leona and Tom's bed, which was salvaged from the church Leona attended as a child. And the pair of brass lamps rescued from a neighbor's curbside trash pile. The shapely lamps now complement the curvy wing chairs in the living room that were gifted by Tom's downsizing parents. "Our home is peaceful and simple," Leona says. "It reflects who we are—literally!"

It also reflects Leona's astute and imaginative eye. She credits her knack for repurposing and vintage style to antiquing with her parents as a child. "They took us to auctions all the time and always pulled over when they saw something potentially interesting on the side of the road," she says. "I definitely got my interest in old things from them."

Architectural salvage and anything with a possibility of being repurposed for functional means call out to Leona. Consider the vintage meat hooks that support hats and bags in the entry, a water well pulley displayed as art over the kitchen fireplace, and the hollow machine mold unearthed in a barn, which Leona turned upside down to create a coffee table. And because she's not a fan of new light fixtures, Leona found and rewired vintage fixtures to use throughout the house.

Still, she wants her home to be an oasis of calm rather than clutter. "I'm not interested in 'stuff' the way I used to be," she says. "My interests have become much more utilitarian."

HOMEY HEARTH Rust-coated urns, salvaged finials, and an old photo of Tom Beck's father as a child, *above left,* form a pretty vignette at the base of the fireplace in the eat-in kitchen. Because the urns didn't have enough patina for Leona, she set them outside to weather a bit. The metal cart, *left,* is one of Leona's favorite possessions. Her father—an auto body shop owner—sprayed the cart with car paint; Leona then cut a maple cutting board to craft its wood top.

SITTING PRETTY
Surrounded by charming architecture, a romantic window seat in the entry hall, *far left,* is plumped with a pillow crafted from an old grain sack.

SIGN OF THE TIMES
Leona dug through a pile of horse barn stall letters at a garage sale to spell out "Beck" above the window, *left.* An existing radiator topped with a tufted cushion creates a convenient spot to slip on shoes, and steel grillwork on the wall makes a clever magnetic memo board.

SLEEK MEETS SALVAGE
Formerly the home's dining room, the new kitchen, *right,* flaunts an industrial vibe that was inspired by a vintage pendant light Leona found at the Brimfield Antique Show in Massachusetts. The sign floating in front of the kitchen window was given to the Becks by Tom's parents.

CALM AND COLLECTED The master bedroom, *this photo,* displays a trove of ingenious retrofits, beginning with the king-size headboard Leona fashioned from the headboard and footboard of her sister's childhood twin bed frame. The bedside tables got a lift courtesy of brass wheels Leona purchased online. The leaded-glass windows were a lucky find; they tuck perfectly into the windows above the bed.

WORKSHOP CHIC
In the corner of her son Jack's bedroom, *left,* Leona situated an industrial workbench as a desk. Large metal trays that may have been used in a commercial kitchen play dual roles as shelves and magnet boards. Leona paid just $10 for the old machinist lamp and had it rewired.

VERSATILE VESSEL
Blue Mason jars, *below left,* make charming vessels for garden cuttings and clothespins in Leona's mudroom. The quaint little containers are found throughout the house, corralling everything from food items to office supplies with old-time flair.

CRISP AND CLEAN
Leona spied the mudroom's trough sink, *below,* in the dirt at a flea market and carted the cast-iron piece home for $90. Mounted on a wall of ceramic white tile, the grand sink plays the vintage part and gets regular use on laundry day and during garden season.

COLLECTIONS

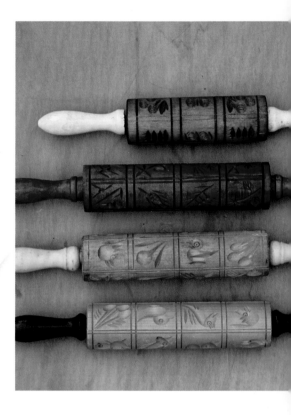

1

PADLOCKS

For their shape and design, padlocks are desirable. But dig deeper and you'll find specific types of locks collectors specialize in: push-key lever locks, story locks, logo locks, military or postal service locks, miniature locks, cut-away locks, or trick locks. Popular brands include Winchester, Sure Grip, Yale, and Excelsior. Many locks corroded over time or were melted during WWII. It's rare to find antique locks with their original key.

2

PRODUCT TINS

To capture the attention of early 1900s shoppers, manufacturers of tobacco, tea, cookies, crackers, coffee, and cocoa, to name a few, would hawk their goods in brightly colored and elaborately designed tins. Sold in both retail shops and by traveling salesmen, tins can be an inexpensive item to collect (many are under $10) and are sought by collectors of vintage advertising and kitchenware.

3

SPRINGERLE MOLDS

Springerle molds look similar to rolling pins but function more like a cookie cutter as they impress designs such as flowers, fruit, or animals onto dough. Dating to 14th-century Germany, the carved wood molds still are used to make traditional holiday anise-flavored springerle cookies. Molds can take the form of rolling pins or flat board presses.

4

VINTAGE TEXTILES

Vintage fabrics, particularly tea towels and feed sacks, attract collectors with their colorful patterns, indispensable function, and rich history. During the Great Depression, flour sacks and feed sacks were often made into tea towels and clothing. Knowing this, savvy flour and feed sack companies adopted more decorative sacks as a ploy to sell their products.

5

HENS ON NESTS

Colorfully painted hens on nests topped many tables in 19th-century England. People were drawn to the hens' decorative outside and the hard-boiled eggs often found inside. Small plain ceramic hens or the later milk glass types typically go for less than $50, but large colorful hens costs hundreds and sometimes even thousands of dollars! The earliest hens weren't marked.

6

SEWING NOTIONS

Notions include all kinds of vintage sewing supplies, such as buttons, beads, trims, lace, and ribbons. Vintage lace and trims were usually made of natural fibers. If an item is synthetic, it's newer. For just a few dollars you can get a card of buttons or a yard of trim or lace from the 1930s and '40s; an intricately beaded appliqué might cost $20.

7

WOOL BLANKETS

Inventions such as the spinning jenny took textile weaving from a cottage industry to a factory-based one. Collectors like Amanda Ficek seek out early to mid-1900s wool blankets bursting with rich color. Popular manufacturers include Pendleton, Hudson Bay, and Faribault.

8

BOARD GAMES

Many 20th-century games are popular for their graphic, hand-painted beauty. The folk art charm runs counter to the slick electronic graphics of today, adding to their sentimental appeal. Expect to pay more for games in excellent condition and for colorful, elaborate designs. Many collectors hang them in a grouping as artwork.

9

DESSERT MOLDS

A staple in American and European kitchens before the first half of the 20th century when they were used for making sculptural salads and desserts, food molds came in a variety of sizes and designs. Today collectors prize copper molds for their pretty sheen, using them more for decoration than dishware. An abundance of stock makes these molds affordable to collect at less than $10 a pop.

10

VINTAGE SUITCASES

As train, auto, and air travel became more accessible, luggage became smaller and more affordable. The hefty steamer trunk gave way to more modern leather, aluminum, and other hard-sided cases like these popular tweed stripe ones. Prices vary with condition and maker.

11

DOG PORTRAITS

Animal portraiture is a sentimental expression of pets as part of the family. In the early 1700s, dog portraits reached their peak during a folk art movement when artists would travel from town to town painting commissions for wealthy families. Now these pooches pepper the walls of canine-loving collectors.

12

LANDSCAPE PAINTINGS

Bartley Johnstone feeds her wanderlust by looking at the landscape paintings that line her walls. "They're a visual escape—a fantasyland my mind can wander into," she says. Flea markets, junk shops, and tag sales are her favorite places for art sleuthing. Her biggest treasure: a torn barn landscape she bought for $15. After having it restored, she discovered it was an American Primitive worth about $3,000.

13

WHIRLIGIGS

These whimsical takes on the weather vane have dotted the countryside since the 1700s. While whirligigs did have some utility, they were essentially for-fun sculptures that have turned into prized folk art collectibles. Both the exposure to weather and the fragile nature of the pieces mean few whirligigs survived over the years.

14

YELLOWWARE

Before the days of Pyrex and plastic, yellowware was all the rage. A type of stoneware defined by the yellow color of clay used, yellowware is glazed clear and can range in color from wheat to soft yellow. The pottery can be plain or decorated with embossed designs or colored slip designs. While bowls are most popular, you can find lidded crocks, mugs, jugs, plates, and even rolling pins.

ROMANTIC

HOMES

Layer on the linen and lace and coat
dreamy white on everything in site.
Add a little sparkle and surfaces drenched
in chippy paint to get to the heart
of this ultrafeminine style.

Simple
BEAUTY

A self-professed Francophile takes
the edge off of her new Illinois home
with weathered flea market finds
collected from near and far.

SUBTLE COLOR The wall color in Tracey Leber's family room, *opposite right*, appears pale green or blue depending on how the sun hits it. The old door leaning against the wall is one of Tracey's most versatile finds because it can be flipped to reveal the blue color on the back. Tracey serves wine from canning jars, *opposite left*, and props an old window frame as art in the dining room. Pale gray paint softened the existing blue-green finish on this flea-found mirror frame, *this photo*. Clothespins hold antique letters purchased in Paris for 2 euros apiece.

F or Tracey Leber's home, blog, and online store, "seeking life's inspirations" is more than just a theme. It's a philosophy that carries her on regular trips to France, where she strolls the flea markets and antiques shops of Paris, Provence, and Normandy seeking treasures for her home-decor store, FrenchLarkspur.com. The store's virtual shelves overflow with well-loved table linens, sheet music, century-old apothecary bottles, hand-scripted letters, and other timeworn items that touch Tracey's heart.

The shop is an extension of Tracey's own style and the look she cultivates in the Chicago-area home she shares with her husband, Steve, and their three children. Although Tracey's style was once modern and urban, the birth of her first child steered her toward a warmer, cozier vibe with European undertones. Today, Tracey's eight-year-old home is alive with vintage patina thanks to crown moldings, antique chandeliers, and architectural salvage culled from expeditions to flea markets, especially the Kane Country Flea Market in St. Charles, Illinois. "In the beginning, I spent my budget on a single large piece each month," Tracey says. "I looked for things that would really affect a room. Once the bones were in place, I looked for smaller vignette items."

A welcoming palette that's mostly white serves as a soothing backdrop for Tracey's melting pot of Scandinavian and French finds. She describes her style as "French Nordic." "I love vintage French decor, but I also love Scandinavian style, with its pale painted furniture and clean lines," Tracey says. "I combine the two."

To warm up her white palette, Tracey adds pops of colors—mostly blues and greens via glass bottles—and she throws in some dark wood pieces among her painted ones. Honey-tone oak flooring also warms rooms from the ground up. "Once I buy a white paint color, I won't use it a second time," she says. "The whites throughout my house are all mix-and-match to avoid a sterile look."

To add another layer to the whites in her home, Tracey seeks out metal chandeliers, clock faces, yellowing pages of old French book spines, and other treasures. "I don't follow any design rules," Tracey says. "I tell people all the time: Decorate with what you love. Don't do anything overly trendy. You'll be happier in the long run."

INFORMAL DINING Wood floors painted gray ground the dining room, *above left.* A mix of chairs gathers around the table, several upholstered with vintage grain sacks—an easy update with a staple gun. Tracey has a knack for spotting the possibilities in the mundane. She asked her husband to build a table, *left,* from the wood pallets her imports are shipped on from Europe. "Originally I wanted it to be an outdoor potting bench, but it looked so pretty inside that it's stayed in the dining room," she says. On the table, mugs hang gracefully from an old bottle drying rack.

DELIGHTFULLY WHITE
Butcher block tops
creamy white cabinets in
the kitchen, *this photo,*
where a vintage library
cart serves as a movable
island. The sink skirt is
fashioned from vintage
linen toweling.

TREASURES ON TASK
Tracey converted a little-used formal living room into a studio and work space, *this photo*. Her three children use the table to do crafts projects and homework. Old baskets, bins, and a wood tool tote corral supplies, and Tracey artfully displays her vintage grain sack collection on a paint-splattered ladder.

Don't be afraid of decorating with whites, even if you have kids.

Tracey has three kids and is a strong believer in decorating with white. Here's why white works: Painted white surfaces don't show dust. Vintage white pieces all have dings already. Slipcovers can be easily washed.

HIT THE RIGHT NOTE
Tracey lets pages of romantic sheet music, *above,* climb the walls in lieu of wallpaper or artwork in the studio. To keep office supplies out of site, she hides them behind simple linen curtains on a tension rod secured to a shelf unit.

NEUTRAL HUES
Daughter Halena's room, *above right,* is anchored by a bed picked up at a garage sale, along with a dresser and vanity, for $100. "It was the most hideous green before I painted it a pale gray," Tracey says. She fashioned a canopy from yards of white netting.

WHOLE NEW PURPOSE
Tracey uses salvaged architectural relics such as weathered window frames throughout the house. This half of an arched window frame, *right,* is embellished with faded French maps, and graciously crowns a small desk made from wood pallets.

TIMELESS STYLE
A vintage picture frame, *below,* calls attention to a trio of old clock faces casually suspended with white ribbon. "Clock faces are hard to find, so when I found a dusty stack in the corner of a vendor's booth, I grabbed them all for $5 each," Tracey says.

CASUAL COMPOSITION
Tracey pairs an old door and suitcases with a painted white dresser and mirror, *right.* She doesn't overthink her vignettes, and once she uses a white paint color, she doesn't use it again. That way, the whites on the walls and furniture are all mix-and-match for more depth.

CAREFREE COLORS
In the master bedroom, *below right,* a serene blue hue accentuates white furniture and breezy bedding. Above the shapely headboard, Tracey props a salvaged window frame on a narrow shelf to create fuss-free and thrifty wall decor.

Seal the Deal

When it comes to old paint, play it safe.

TOP IT OFF: As much as she loves original patina, when it comes to living with old pieces, Tracey is careful to seal chipping paint with polyurethane, especially if the piece is going in a child's room. And if going in the kitchen or dining room, a food-safe sealer is used.

SPECIAL TOUCHES
Mercury glass candlesticks add sparkle atop a farm-table desk, *this photo.* Standing in for artwork, pages from a French play dangle from a rescued window frame. "The French have a love of making everyday living special. Their style is laid-back and about enjoying life," Tracey says.

Secondhand
CHIC

With a discerning eye and a creative approach, a Connecticut designer makes old things new again in a delightfully modern way.

PERSONAL TOUCH Interior designer Maureen Mazur-Fawcett, *opposite*, rarely buys decorative elements online. "I need to hold a piece so I can feel its weight and study its patina," she says. Soft pink draperies provide a billowy backdrop for the living room, *this photo*. The set of four lined, pleated panels would cost upward of $1,500 if custom-made, but Maureen paid less than $100 for them at a local flea market. The coffee table, with inlaid wood panels, was a $200 tag sale find.

Some people like crosswords, others prefer chess. For Connecticut interior designer Maureen Mazur-Fawcett, flea market shopping is the ultimate mind-bending game. "I'm most excited when I see a piece that gets my creative juices flowing," Maureen says. "I'll stare at it and ask, 'How can I make this work for me?' I'm constantly amazed by how many new and unusual uses I can come up with for a single find."

Maureen sees tabletops where others see doors, and marble mantels are reimagined as wall shelves and cheese boards. With the exception of milk glass and pressed glass, Maureen rarely hunts for knickknacks. Instead she scours flea markets, church sales, and salvage yards for large-scale items capable of lending grand presence to a room. Architectural elements like pillars, corbels, millwork, and ironwork rank high on her list of favorite finds, as well as garden relics that she reinvents for indoor use.

Never one to shy away from a little wear, Maureen believes the rustier and crustier the better. "Perfection doesn't appeal to me," she says. "I would rather have something that's worn and has a story." Sometimes she even speeds up the aging process by buffing shiny metal with gilder's wax or leaving interior decor outdoors to naturally oxidize.

Despite Maureen's passion for all things old, the aesthetic in her Ridgefield, Connecticut, home is remarkably modern thanks to a fresh take on color. Rooms swathed in crisp white paint create a quiet, gallerylike setting where Maureen's thoughtfully curated collections become the art. Various pastels, such as the whisper-soft pink blush of the cotton draperies in the living room and the sage green seats in the dining room, feel serene thanks to a host of edgy accents, such as Lucite-backed counter stools, a zebra-stripe rug, and a cattle skull complete with horns.

"Sophisticated flea market style is a well-balanced mix of textures, time periods, and high-low decor," Maureen says. "It can only be achieved by careful editing and undecorating, which is ironic considering that people wrongly associate it with musty houses overflowing with superfluous stuff." Maureen's design philosophy is definitely "less is more." She doesn't buy just to buy or collect for the sake of collecting. "I surround myself with things that have purpose and meaning, and it results in a very special, personal style," she says.

PERFECT PATINA The old French cabinet with chicken wire doors, *above left,* was found at a junk shop. Other than fixing a broken leg, Maureen left the piece as is. "I love original paint," she says. "It's part of the life of the piece and part of its story." On the porch, a slatted-top coffee table flaunts its original green patina, *left.* Tucked underneath is Maureen's collection of Hudson Valley River rocks in a carved oak bowl. On the wall hangs a framed headstone rubbing Maureen found in England. "They don't let you do that anymore," she says. "I was thrilled to find one of this scale."

GARDEN INSPIRED
Her breakfast room at one end of the porch, *this photo,* features a table Maureen made by topping two cast-iron urns with an old plank door found at a salvage yard. She scored the suite of vintage Italian side chairs from a local consignment shop. "Anyone can go to a furniture store or open a catalog and buy a dining table, but using different found elements makes any piece one-of-a-kind," Maureen says.

WHITE ON WHITE

In keeping with her clean, classic style, Maureen installed white subway tiles above the kitchen countertops, *above left,* creating a clean canvas for her mix of old and new white dishware. The vintage wood drying rack adds a warm tone to the space.

LIGHT THE WAY

At the far end of the kitchen, *left,* Maureen hung a narrow shelf on iron brackets in front of the windows, providing light for plants as well as a landing pad for her mortar and pestle collection, old books, and other flea market treasures.

CLEVER CONSTRUCTION

The pot rack, *above,* was made using plumbing fixtures from a local big-box store. The antique leaded-glass doors with a charming oval motif were old windows Maureen found at a salvage yard, and became the perfect alternative to run-of-the-mill cabinet doors.

Trust Your Intuition

Don't let unique treasures get away.

I'LL TAKE IT: While you can't buy everything you find, Maureen believes if it catches your eye and you find it intriguing, you should take it home. Even if you don't have a use for it at the moment it might become the inspiration for something else.

SQUARED AWAY

In the kitchen, *above,* Maureen hung two Art Deco pendant lights. She found the vintage globes at a junk shop in Hudson Valley and installed new fittings. Originally from a ballroom ceiling in Argentina, the vintage glass tiles behind the range now create an artful backsplash.

AT YOUR SERVICE

For both their function and beauty, Maureen collects silver-plate platters, *left,* snatching them up from estate sales and thrift shops whenever she can. She uses them to ground candles and other tabletop essentials or as chargers when serving food. "Their shine adds a little bit of glam to anything," she says.

WORDS OF WISDOM
In the master bedroom, *this photo,* Maureen enhanced a reproduction trumeau mirror with a self-adhering decal bearing an inspirational message. In front of the mirror stands a vintage bergère chair wearing terry cloth upholstery.

Everyday holds a possibility of a Miracle

A FRESH FACE
Identical chests flank Maureen's bed, *left.* "It's very rare to find original pairs in a flea market, so when I spotted these, I didn't hesitate to jump on them," she says. She looked past the thick black paint coating the pieces, knowing she would strip them and refinish with a white wash.

ON THE RISE The vintage porcelain pedestal sink in the powder room, *below left,* was the right scale for the tight space, but its height didn't measure up to Maureen's nearly 6-foot frame. Ingeniously, she secured a glass ball from a wine decanter to the base of the pedestal to give the petite sink a step up.

FRAME OF MIND
In her home studio, *below,* Maureen created a gallery wall by framing her sons' artwork in simple white frames. In lieu of a traditional desk, she mounted a pair of large salvaged corbels to the wall and topped them with custom-cut tempered glass.

A Worn
WELCOME

A home in a historic Texas
town proves that good
planning and authentic details
can give even a new house
instant patina.

STAYING NEUTRAL Grouped for greater impact on the salvaged mantel, a collection of mercury glass, *opposite top*, adds a warm glow to the room. Angie Cavalier and daughter Annie, *opposite bottom*, relax with the pooches on a back patio that sees year-round use. Without texture, an all neutral room would feel cold and bare rather than serene, so adding nubby fabrics, sisal, weathered woods, and stone in the living room, *this photo*, does the trick.

A ngie Cavalier remembers her grandmother's house in Fort Worth had glass doorknobs on every door. Such fancy, old-fashioned touches caught Angie's young eye and years later inspired her and her husband, Michael, to build an "old" home of their own.

Like the doorknobs, small but meaningful details give the interiors well-aged character. Set against a white palette that provides a soft, almost dreamy quality, the textures of old paint, rough linen, and warm wood give this new house the authentic look of a home from Angie's grandmother's day. "Every room in the house is painted the same shade of white," Angie says. "When you have a lot of texture, it really works."

The Cavaliers had built new homes before, but designing a house to look old was a new experience with plenty of challenges as well as many rewards. Fortunately, Angie had been preparing for this challenge her whole life, ripping scores of inspirational photos from magazines and catalogs ever since she was a child.

Those photos gave the architect clear direction from the outset. Angie knew, for instance, she wanted a claw-foot tub with exposed plumbing in the middle of the master bath. And the master bedroom needed a step-up reading niche flooded with light through wood-trimmed windows.

Additional inspiration came from flea market and antiques store finds, which Angie started collecting even before the building began. Eventually, the Cavaliers' garage and two rented storage spaces overflowed with chandeliers, furnishings, architectural relics, and other treasures. One of those purchases—a supply of reclaimed pine flooring—is integral to the home's overall character. Salvaged from an old factory in the Midwest, the Cavaliers had the planks planed, sanded, and waxed, laying a foundation of warmth for the house.

The floor's rich tones balance the home's soothing palette. Materials such as beaded board and ceiling tin bestow touches of charm from another era. Furnishings that were designed for formal use have developed a more casual, worn feel over time. It all adds up to the genuine article—a house that doesn't just look old but bears pieces of history everywhere you look. The house even creaks—an unexpected detail, Angie says, that undoubtedly would make her grandmother smile.

AGED ELEGANCE Nubby and textural linens dress classic furniture, *above left,* to create the mix of formal and well-worn casual that Angie is partial to. "I love anything imperfect," she says. Leaded-glass windows topped with a salvaged ledge and old botanical prints round out the look in this corner of the living room. The dining room table, *left,* came from a French sewing factory and is pocked with the needle marks to prove it. "They give a pretty texture to the top," Angie says. White French chairs with signs of wear lend a delicate counterbalance to the dark table and warm pine floors.

CONVERSATION PIECES
A counter from a candy store in Pennsylvania now serves as a kitchen island, *far left,* complete with a new marble top. "More than anything else in the house, that's the piece people talk about," Angie says. Also of note: an antique chandelier, old tobacco-leaf baskets, and reclaimed leaded-glass cabinet doors.

DISH IT OUT Originally a fixture in a Texas general store, the hutch is exactly how Angie found it. Its size suits the dining room's small scale yet provides ample space for her English transferware, *left.*

IN THE BALANCE
Continuing the play of rustic and refined, an old American scale, *right,* sits atop a sleek marble counter near the porcelain sink. An old hanging English cupboard is filled with a collection of ironstone.

SWEET DREAMS The master bedroom, *this photo,* radiates true romantic style. The iron bed was custom-made to replicate an antique Angie saw in a magazine. The bedside table was fashioned from an iron factory base and a wood top. To complete the scene, an old boot bench, mantel piece, and architectural brackets, complete with chippy paint, join delicate bed linens and a glamorous chandelier.

LET THERE BE WHITE
Timeworn touches fill the master bath, *left,* including salvaged wainscoting, molding, and doors. The room's all-white color scheme produces a spa-like atmosphere that stands ready to pamper. A wall of vintage mirrors reflects light and adds sparkle.

STOW AWAY
A pale wood armoire with metal trim, *below left,* dates to the 1800s and offers plenty of storage. Traces of white in the crevices hint that it was once painted. Stacked on top, vellum and leather suitcases from Europe bear initials from former travelers.

EASY ELEGANCE
A mirror framed in salvaged molding, *below,* counters the smooth marble vanity top and floor surfaces. Angie made the petite pendant lights from old glass lampshades. A vast shell collection fills an old display case, adding texture and a nod to seaside style.

COLLECTIONS

1

BRASS CANDLESTICKS

In the 18th and 19th centuries, candlesticks were common in the household. Because brass was less expensive than silver or gold, it was often used. Early examples were braised together but later, candlesticks were cast from molds. Expect to pay up to $1,500 for an early stick. Or shop for a newer one for less than $200. Amass your collection, mixing sizes, styles, and eras to show off the variety.

2

FASHION FINDS

Vintage clothes and accessories lend romantic charm and are readily available on the secondhand market. Look for picturesque apparel in good, clean condition without odors. Costume jewelry is a thriftier option than gemstones and precious metals. Display finds on an old dress form, which can be found for $100 to $400. Test the mechanisms before buying to make sure they work.

3

VINTAGE BOOKS

With just about any collectible, quality and condition are desired and determine the item's value. That goes for antique book collectors as well, but if collecting books as decorative objects to establish a romantic style, buyers seek well-worn books. Look for tattered, yellowing pages and books with missing covers exposing the stitched binding. You can often pick them up for next to nothing.

4

IRONSTONE

Born in early 1800 England, ironstone contains no iron and was typically decorated. In the 1940s durable and affordable white ironstone was attractive to rural American families and often embossed with agricultural motifs. American potters began to make whiteware in the 1950s. Graniteware, stoneware, pearl china, and feldspar china are often synonymous with the term *ironstone*.

5

EMBROIDERED LINENS

Once a symbol of wealth and status, embroidered table linens were often adorned with intricate designs and monograms of the owner. Treasured for their craftsmanship, the linens' value often comes from accessing the rarity and difficulty of pattern, quality of work, and overall condition. Sets are highly sought after.

6

POCKET WATCHES

Pocket watches served as a portable time device and a fashion statement. During the industrial revolution, mass-produced clock components made them affordable to the working class. In fact, railroad pocket watches are particularly sought after. Look for pieces made by Ball, Hamilton, Illinois, Waltham, Elgin, and Hampden.

7

ETCHED STEMWARE

The interest in fresh and pretty glassware means colored etched stemware from the 1930s to the '50s is attracting attention. Popular U.S. manufacturers include Cambridge, Heisey, Fostoria, and Tiffin. Look for it at garage sales, auctions, and secondhand shops.

8

BIRDCAGES

The popularity of keeping birds as pets reached its height in 1900 America, and decorative cages were an important element of a civilized parlor. The Andrew B. Hendryx Co. offered many styles and sizes of brass, bronze, and japanned birdcages, which are now prized by collectors.

9

ARCHITECTURAL SALVAGE

In an effort to save building treasures from the landfill, 1980s architectural enthusiasts began making deals with demolition firms to save tile, millwork, doors, mantels, hardware, and more so they might be reused. The history, intrigue, and beauty of salvaged items appeals to decorators and collectors.

ROMANTIC

10

SILVER PLATE

Silver-plated tableware from the early 20th century offered elegance without breaking the bank. Made of a thin layer of sterling silver bonded over a metal, such as copper or nickel, silver plate is more affordable than sterling silver. Most collectors don't polish the patina as they prefer the tarnished look.

11

OLD PHOTOS

Scarcity, condition, and the identity of the photographer and subject all help determine the value of vintage photos. Collectors often seek a certain category—portraits, landscapes, animals, architecture—and prefer originals to reprints though they are much more costly.

12

VINTAGE MIRRORS

In 16th-century Italy, the Venetians perfected glass and metal mirrors. Made in every imaginable shape, some mirrors were adorned with etched motifs. While some old mirrors are frameless, a mirror's frame may be just as appealing to collectors as the mirror itself.

13

HOME MAGAZINES

In the 19th century, women started turning to magazines for information about their homes and gardens. Today, as digital versions threaten their favorite printed companions, collectors are drawn to the colorful illustrations and graphic covers of early issues. Whole magazines and single pages from dealers such as Michael Gallagher range from a few bucks up to $50.

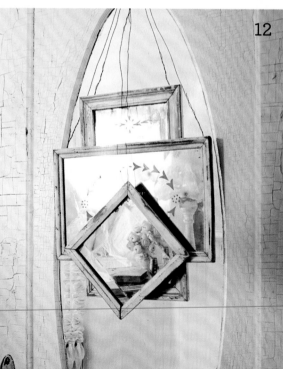

14

AUTOGRAPH BOOKS

Popular during the Victorian period, autograph books or albums were traditionally exchanged among friends and colleagues to fill with signatures, poems, drawings, and personal messages. Many are horizontal in format and bound in everything from cardboard to gold-tooled leather.

MODERN

HOMES

Dial back the clock and give midcentury style
another run. Sleek, sculptural furnishings
and bold, graphic patterns reflective of the era
give any room a cool retro vibe.

Masterful MIXING

Streamlined midcentury modern pieces combined with glamorous Hollywood Regency overtures lend this Nashville home a breezy, welcoming quality.

MODERN ASSEMBLY Homeowner Brandy Adams loves a little bling. In her dining room, *opposite,* she displays vintage brass objects and drinkware with gold accents. A 1960s credenza found on eBay nestles in a nook next to the fireplace in Brandy's living room, *this photo.* The midcentury geometric art print and a brass-and-wood lamp serve as period-appropriate companions. "When I saw the lamp, I had to have it," Brandy says. "It's the perfect mix of clean lines and glam."

W hen Brandy Adams thinks of vintage decor, she envisions cool stuff, but she knows that for some people, *vintage* brings to mind the words *cheap* and *junky*. If those naysayers stepped inside her Nashville-area home, however, they'd be in for a surprise. Rooms are sleek, sophisticated, and current—despite most of the furniture and accessories being plucked from estate sales, flea markets, and thrift stores. "A contractor once came in and said, 'Your house looks very California,'" Brandy says. "That's the beauty of vintage. There are so many directions you can take it."

Since moving in four years ago, Brandy, who runs the online store Make + Model, has given her 1970s home a carefree vibe suited to family life (she and her husband, Judson, have two children, ages 10 and 8). Brandy painted walls white to brighten rooms and create a clean canvas for geometric patterns and vintage finds, some of which provide the bright pops of aqua and orange she loves. The clean-lined midcentury modern pieces she prefers aren't too fussy. Then again, she didn't want her home to look like a set from *Mad Men*, either. Hence the curvy and glamorous vintage pieces mixed in with new items from mainstream retailers. "I don't think you can have everything just one way," Brandy says. "If everything in a home is vintage or antique, it will look dated."

Still, for Brandy, it is the vintage items that give rooms their soul. She can envision a group of lawyers from the 1950s hammering out business in a conference room while sitting on the leather chairs now pulled up to her dining table. And the "you're my goddess" note from a boyfriend to his girlfriend that she found taped to the bottom of a molded candle was enough to pique her interest in the $7 lady "sculpture" that's now displayed on her living room's built-in buffet. "My love for vintage is not only finding the pieces, but investigating who made them," she says. "It's the history—the story—I'm attracted to."

The desire for more great stories keeps Brandy making the flea market rounds. Her family knows anything in their house today could end up for sale on Brandy's online store tomorrow. "I'm someone who just has to constantly be creating and moving things around," Brandy says. "I would never want my house to be finished."

METALLIC ACCENTS Solid brass fishlike andirons, *left,* bring an ornate touch to the living room's simple brick fireplace, which Brandy painted white. Brandy, *above left,* sits on one of her feel-good favorite finds—a Lucite-and-brass barstool. Brandy "window shops" online to familiarize herself with upscale vintage items so she's prepared to snatch up a garage sale or estate sale gem.

LET IT SHINE High-gloss black paint and mirrored shelves push a vintage rattan bar cart, *far left,* into the 21st century. The vintage Stiffel lamp (one of a pair) was a $25 thrift store bargain—they're worth about $3,500!

PULLING IT TOGETHER A chrome-base Hollywood Regency dining set, *left,* was a $200 flea market steal. The '70s carved stone chess set provides Brandy's signature burst of color, while brass lamps from the 1960s deliver sparkle on the built-in buffet, which Brandy found at a Habitat for Humanity store.

LUXE YET LIVABLE The living room's seating pieces are all vintage bargains, jazzed up by a new animal print rug, *right.* Brandy reupholstered the Billy Baldwin tuxedo sofa from the 1950s and formed a love seat by pushing together two '70s chairs, which she found for $25 each. "I was going for that lounging feel," she says. Teal chairs from the 1940s give the room its color pop. "This is my haven," Brandy says.

Lacquer It

Lacquered finishes give Brandy Adams' vintage pieces a modern edge.

CHOOSE PAINT Brandy uses Rust-Oleum's professional latex paint and an airless sprayer to provide a smooth finish without the extra cleanup and odor of oil-base paint.

CONSIDER SHEEN Opt for paints with either a high-gloss or satin finish. "Some pieces look more sophisticated and expensive when done in a lower sheen, while others need the pop of high gloss," Brandy says. Determine the sheen based on the piece, its purpose, and the color being used. A high-gloss sheen, for example, gives high-use items more durability.

CALL THE PROS Brandy lacquers small pieces on her own, but has a cabinetmaker or painter professionally finish large ones. "They're used to working with wood and getting it in perfect condition for that high-lacquer finish," she says. She has used an auto body shop, but has found that they are best for outdoor metal pieces.

PULL UP A CHAIR
Brandy snapped up six midcentury black leather chairs originally used in an attorney's office for her dining room, *left.* "They're masculine, but also have a feminine look because of their curves," she says. The white Panton chairs are reproductions.

ORANGE CRUSH
A 1960s faux-bamboo cabinet, *above,* looks fresh and fun lacquered in bright orange. A chinoiserie garden stool takes things back to traditional. "I always mix the old with the new to give my spaces depth and personality," Brandy says.

A TOUCH OF GLAM
The brass étagère, *right,* in the dining room is from the 1970s. "They're starting to be sought after," Brandy says. "Brass is so hot right now." She found this one at an antiques store. The glass shelves and metallic finish reflect light to make this corner really shine.

STEP-BY-STEP
Brandy updated a 1950s bench in her foyer, *below,* with white paint and faux leather. The salvaged sign, from a New Orleans hotel, actually lights up. Graphic wallpaper and an ornate mirror in the stairwell reflect Brandy's love of bold pattern and mixing design styles a little at a time.

LIVING LARGER
Continuing a streamlined look in the master bedroom, *right,* Brandy began with a canvas of white from floor to ceiling to make the small sitting area seem larger. A vintage Lucite-and-glass coffee table, an estate sale purchase along with the sofa, almost fades away on the flokati rug.

BLACK ACCENTS
In Brandy's master bathroom, *below right,* she used a pair of black framed oval mirrors and faucets to add a touch of class to the basic double sink vanity, which she painted bright white like the walls. The ultramodern pendant lights continue the room's symmetry.

WITHOUT SKIPPING A BEAT
Geometric vinyl wallpaper and
modern bedding, *this photo,* lend
10-year-old Pierce's bedroom a
groovy attitude. For an offbeat
bedside table, Brandy bought a
drum from an antiques mall and
topped it with tempered glass. "I find
inspiration everywhere," she says.

Timeless CLASSIC

A San Diego stylist fills his modern home with family heirlooms, vintage collections, and fanciful finds that pay tribute to his heritage and hobbies.

M oving to a 1952 midcentury modern ranch required Paul Scott Silvera to journey to a design era he was not overly familiar with. Yet the transition from a 1930s bungalow to his new digs in San Diego has proved seamless, thanks to his classic aesthetic, which reflects his history and the life he shares with his partner, Todd Schultz. "My style tends to be bungalow, but I found I could still layer things from our families and travels in this modern interior," Paul says. "The vintage things create a more natural look. If I used only midcentury things, it would appear forced."

Paul knows a thing or two about creating artistically assembled interiors. He owns Scout @ Quarters D, a retail, design, and home-staging business that finds him traveling both domestically and abroad in search of furniture and accessories for his clients and his shop—and while he's there, for his own home as well. "You are always best at what you're passionate about," Paul says. "I am passionate about collecting and decorating, so there's a synergy with my business."

Through the years Paul has hauled home an array of objects. His collections include antique walking sticks, retro cameras, fly-fishing reels, vintage coat hangers, and hotel ashtrays. "I am a hunter and gatherer," Paul says. "My style evolves as I am introduced to new places, textures, and colors. When I travel, I always go to neighborhoods where there are likely to be flea markets or estate sales."

Paul looks for furniture with sculptural presence such as his living room chair. "It reminds me of a vintage yacht," he says. "The carvings look a bit like an anchor chain made from teak." He also hunts for items to assemble into captivating displays like the monkey sketch he arranged with family photos and other ephemera in the living room. A master of displaying, Paul suggests giving treasures room to breathe. "Group collections in an orderly fashion so the viewer can see and understand individual items. Pare down groupings when they start to look cluttered," he says.

His home's streamlined architecture—along with walls and woodwork strategically painted the same shade of tan—allows Paul's treasures to take center stage. "Our home is a great showcase because it's open and light," he says. "The neutral backdrops let my things be the stars."

PICTURE PERFECT Color comes quietly to the home Paul shares with his partner, Todd Schultz. A 1950s bird-figure mosaic, green-glass electrical insulators, vintage books, and blue pottery bowls hang out with rustic driftwood and shiny accents on shelves in the dining room, *above left*. A 19th-century French iron bust and ceramic dachshund act as unexpected bookends. A large portrait, *left*, is anchored by a stack of vintage tweed suitcases. The photo was enlarged from the original 12×8-inch photo Paul found in a store in Germany, unframed and rolled up in a corner.

Transitional-style Parsons chairs, *this photo,* and a simple pedestal table provide function in streamlined fashion in the dining room. The area rug is crafted of shapes cut from Persian and Chinese Art Deco rugs, which were stitched together and overdyed in indigo.

Beauty in Black and White

Grace walls with art and artifacts sporting little or no color..

WALL POWER: Though classic staples, think beyond black and white photographs and search for duo tone charcoal drawings, pen and ink, etchings, and typography to make statements on your walls.

A TAILORED FIT
Paul bought the guest bedroom's bed and dresser in Scotland, *far left*. He previously used them in his 1930s bungalow, proving that fine antiques work equally well in contemporary and classic interiors. The painting above the bed reflects Paul's passion for sailing.

HAND-ME-DOWNS
The painting in the master suite, *left,* was found in Todd's mom's attic, and the Heywood Wakefield nightstands and mirror belonged to his grandmother. The bench at the foot of the bed was upholstered with canvas tarp featuring a tattered silhouette.

WELL TRAVELED
Mirrors from Scotland, *above,* and a lifesaving instructional chart found in London hang above a French Art Deco dresser in the guest bedroom. The 1950s Tour de France cyclist figures found in Belgium pair with a 1920s taxi light bought for $75 at a Brooklyn flea market.

Personal TOUCH

With color and creativity at every turn, this Nashville home is a purposeful reflection of what family members truly love and how they live.

THE PLAYING FIELD Gen and Ben Sohr and children Lucy and Oden, *opposite bottom,* have all gotten into the collecting game. "The kids both appreciate the hunt and the fun of it," Gen says. Card and board games, *opposite top,* are also favorite family pastimes as evident on tables throughout the house. The thrifted sofa in the playroom, *this photo,* isn't one Gen would naturally snap up, but the stunning chrome legs were too much to resist, so she reupholstered it in a patterned fabric to give it a custom feel. A seagrass rug, loose Roman shades, and colorful accessories keep the space casual.

There's no such thing as just another day at the office for Gen and Ben Sohr. At 10 p.m. they're perched at their kitchen island going over plans for a construction project. The couple's business, which designs, builds, and renovates houses and develops retail spaces, is based out of their light-filled cottage in a historic Nashville neighborhood. When the couple built the house on the foundation of a late-1800s home that was falling apart, they included work spaces for each of them. But blueprints and swatches often spill into other areas of the home.

Though they couldn't save the original house, the couple incorporated a salvaged stair banister and fireplace mantel and included architectural details indicative of older homes—tall moldings, ceiling beams, wood floors, and double-hung windows. "We have traditional roots, but there's a modern take on everything we do, a sense of whimsy and color," Gen says.

The Sohrs moved from San Francisco in 2003 to raise their children closer to family. Most of the walls in their home are gleaming white—all the better to bounce around natural light and put the spotlight on the couple's modern-leaning furniture, fabulous artwork, and eye-popping flea-found accessories. "For us, white is a signature element because it feels really clean and can be modern," Gen says. "When you love vintage the way we do it needs a clean environment. The white background makes the vintage pieces stand out, makes them feel fresh, makes them the hero."

The duo's collections run the gamut, from vintage with a pricey pedigree to classic and free items. But they're always sprinkled among new items. Just as she doesn't wear an entirely vintage outfit, she doesn't outfit her home with all vintage finds.

"Everyone's home is a reflection of the people who inhabit the space," Gen says. "I think our home tells a story about us—that we love to hunt down a great vintage treasure, that we are not scared of color or to mix patterns, and that we are a creative and upbeat family."

STRIKE A BALANCE

The black-and-white paintings, *opposite,* are flea market finds that strike a balance with the living room's traditional architecture and symmetrical arrangement. "When you find a pair of anything you love, you should buy them," Gen says. The leather love seats are her favorite flea finds ever, and in a home full of superlative scores, that's saying a lot!

SET THE SCENE A

ceramic side table, *far left,* sidles up to a vintage Bertola chair and a salvaged signage number. Gen and Ben rely on their experience designing clothing stores to make arrangements that mix material, shape, and color.

EASYGOING EATERY

A ceramic pendant light snapped up at a South Beach flea market in Florida illuminates the breakfast nook, *above left,* which defines comfort thanks to the mix-and-don't-match chairs and pillow-plumped banquette.

FIRST IMPRESSIONS

One exception to the Sohrs' mostly white walls is the front entry, *left,* where a sandy-hue floral wallpaper greets guests and takes kindly to accents of blue and orange. The white lacquered pedestal table was beat up and wood-stained before getting a glamorous makeover.

SEEING RED To get a prep kitchen feel, the Sohrs created an oversize island, *this photo,* loaded with big baskets. Gen's signature tomato-red color jumps to the foreground on a trio of metal stools in the mostly white kitchen. Gen gravitates toward the daring hue for its youthfulness and exuberance, and it makes an appearance all over the house in varying degrees.

BUDDING ARTISTS
Many of the kids' doodles and projects wind up on this gallery wall in Gen's home office, *left,* where she selects pieces based on a unifying color scheme—all contain red, blue, tan, or white. Then Gen relies on understated and inexpensive frames to showcase the pieces.

CREATION STATIONS
Creative spaces, *below left,* abound in the Sohr home and inspiration is plentiful. When arranging wall art, Gen doesn't make herself crazy with measuring. "Start with the big pieces," she says. "Put them at eye level, and then cover the entire space. Just eyeball it."

LAST-MINUTE DEAL
Oden's room hosts a well-worn bamboo desk, *below,* that Gen nabbed for $25 at a San Francisco flea market. One of Gen's flea tips: Go late on the last day. You may miss the super-coveted pieces, but you'll find quirky things and vendors will be ready to make deals so they don't have to pack it up.

Edit, edit, edit. That's design-speak for limiting displays to just a few standouts.

Gen uses trade secrets from retail merchandising to create attention-grabbing vignettes. Remembering that less is more is one philosophy that will keep your home from looking like a disheveled clearance rack.

MIXED MEDIA

The master bedroom, *above left,* heralds eclectic style where an arched headboard offers a neutral backdrop for patterned bedding and a vintage marquee letter pairs with a flea market portrait. Gen's favorite color is vivid red-orange, so she fell hard for the lacquered Asian-style side table.

DRESSED FOR SUCCESS

A light-drenched niche in Gen's dressing room, *left,* includes a curvy, knobby-leg table she found at a thrift store. A shiny white ceramic garden stool and a pair of mirrors bounce ample light around the space, and wall hooks provide grab-and-go convenience for necklaces and bracelets.

FINISHING TOUCHES

Rather than stash her eye-catching jewelry out of sight, Gen uses it to add color and personality to her dressing table, *above.* She gathers the accessories on decorative trays, pretty plates, and even objects like this ceramic horse, which makes selecting baubles a snappy task.

COLLECTIONS

1

COCKTAIL NAPKINS

Fun and cheeky, cocktail napkins provide a snapshot of mid-20th-century life. Collectors snatch them up and actually put the mixed and matched napkins to use when hosting gatherings. Most are unsigned, but you might happen across a napkin signed by a designer, such as iconic artist Vera Neumann. Find individual napkins for as low as 50 cents or look for coveted sets of eight for $15 to $150.

2

GLASS ART

William John Blenko started producing decorative glassware in his West Virginia plant in the 1920s. All manner of transparent, handblown Blenko pieces in a rainbow of hues and styles are now collected by enthusiasts. The distinctive modern lines of pieces from the 1950s through the 1970s are some of the most prized by collectors.

3

RADIOS

Popular radio manufacturers include RCA, Philco, Zenith, and Emerson. Vintage radios can be identified by model number, and many collectors seek them purely for decoration, not expecting them to work. The 1920s brought elaborate designs, and Art Deco styles of the '30s and '40s were often made of Bakelite and other early resins or plastics.

4

SIGNAGE & TYPOGRAPHY

Collectors seek typography in many forms from printed pieces to signs that once graced marquees and storefronts. Vintage signs can be underappreciated works of art because many early sign painters were, in fact, artists. Original handmade signs and individual letters or numbers are popular as are newer pre-1940s ones made of steel and baked-on porcelain.

5

LAMPS

Decorative table lamps reached the height of their popularity at the beginning of the 20th century with Arts and Crafts and Art Nouveau styles. Post-WWII lamps gave way to a simpler, space-age feel with decorated parchment or fiberglass shades with various bases fashioned from ceramic, iron, brass, and wood.

6

CAMERAS

From 19th-century wood cameras to classic vintage Leicas to instant Polaroid in the 1940s, cameras continue to intrigue collectors for their aesthetics and technological innovation. With George Eastman's 1880s invention of Kodak film, cameras got smaller, and further advancements made photography more practical and affordable.

7

GLOBES

Vintage globes are appealing for their beauty and geographic history. Most globes are not stamped with a date, so collectors like Scott Johnson examine country boundary lines to help determine a general era. Produced between the 1880s and 1970s, the oldest feature paper maps overlaid on wood, metal, or plaster spheres.

8

METAL FANS

In the 1920s, General Electric released a fan design crafted from aluminum, which appealed to the residential market since it was quieter and less expensive than steel. Later Emerson Electric released the model most familiar to today's consumers. Vintage fans sell for $25 to upward of $500.

9

ASHTRAYS

The first ashtrays appeared in the mid-19th century with widespread popularity of smoking. Though smoking has fallen out of vogue, these vessels remain in demand. Typically made from metal, ceramic, or glass, ashtrays span many eras and are found in an array of designs, including simple geometrics, ornate, and novelty. They range in value from high-end designer to mass-produced advertising grade.

MODERN

10

MCCOY POTTERY

McCoy began making its famous art pottery nearly a century ago and reached its peak in the 1950s, producing its most sought-after cookie jars. Launched in 1961, the Harmony line typified modernity with simple lines, free-flowing design, and retro hues like this aqua blue.

11

MODERN SCARVES

Collectors can't resist a fashionable scarf bearing bold motifs and the distinct signature of the designer, like these from Vera Neumann. Snag a Vera for under $10; prices go up if the signature is small (her early days) or if the design has a ladybug (a sign that Vera herself, not a staffer, designed it).

12

GLASS MARBLES

The era of shooting marbles has come and gone, but the swirled pretties live on. Collectors covet German handmade glass marbles from the 1800s: A single one can go for about $50. But they also have a nostalgic soft spot for machine-made marbles from the 1900s. Score jars of marbles for a few dollars at garage sales, and display a colorful mix in clever ways like this gum-ball machine.

13

FIESTA DINNERWARE

Introduced in 1936 by the Homer Laughlin Pottery Co., Fiesta dinnerware was casual and inexpensive. It's known for its Art Deco aesthetic and bold colors that were meant to be mixed and matched. The original line consisted of red, cobalt, green, yellow, and ivory. A slew of other fun colors followed. "Colors and trademarks help determine value, along with condition," says collector McKenzie Wyatt.

METAL CHAIRS

Chairs of all eras can be popular collectibles, but midcentury lovers seek the sleek lines of modern seating as found in these metal garden chairs. Sets are difficult to score so look for single chairs of similar make and color to pair together indoors or out.

PROJECTS
FOR YOUR HOME

Let your imagination soar with pages of inspiring projects. See how reclaimed relics are remade and reinvented into fresh home decor worthy of bragging rights and star status.

What a Gem

These organizers let pretty jewels take center stage.

When displayed like this, jewelry becomes a fashion statement for your room, plus it's organized and easily accessible. Cut old aluminum radiator sheeting to fit in a frame and screw to the back of frame to secure. Tiny S hooks can help hang necklaces and bracelets. Slide bangles onto a paper towel holder and corral other baubles on a tiered serving tray or in small dishes.

Silver Lining

Let lustrous metallic finishes frame family photos.

Treasured photographs deserve a frame as original as they are. Find silver or silver-accented tableware and mirrors to use as frames, then photo copy and cut photos to fit, using double-sided tape to mount them. Adhere a hanger to the back using epoxy.

TIP: These same objects work just as well to showcase new or vintage artwork, too.

The Great Divide

Add a bit of privacy without blocking the view.

Suspended from a porch beam, vintage window frames create a pretty trellis. Remove glass and arrange the frames on the ground to fit in the porch opening, allowing several inches between each frame. Attach the top frames to the beam or ceiling using screw eyes and S hooks, making sure the frames hang level. Continue hanging frames together with screw eyes and S hooks, securing the bottom frame to the floor using screw eyes and hook binders to limit movement of the trellis.

TIP: To prevent old window frames from splitting, drill pilot holes before adding screw eyes.

Spring Fever

Perk up plain glass vases by adding metal coils.

Rusty springs with industrial pasts make interesting "sleeves" for vases. Look for springs at farm sales and salvage yards. Those wearing chippy paint are particularly popular. Spray springs with a clear sealer to protect from further rusting or paint loss. Place a small vase or jar inside, and fill with water and favorite booms.

TIP: To prevent metal springs from scratching delicate surfaces, cut felt strips to fit underneath the spring and attach using hot glue.

Eye Candy

Pretty paint colors give little bottles or jars a big boost.

You can customize a vase collection from simple glass containers. Clean the bottle inside and out with warm soapy water and let dry. Prime the interior by pouring rubbing alcohol into the bottle and swirling to coat the inside surface. Pour out excess and let dry. Pour enamel glass paint into bottle, tapping and swirling to coat entire surface. Pour out excess paint, then place bottle upside down on a paper towel to dry, occasionally removing excess paint as it pools at the opening.

Page by Page

Set book illustrations free as whimsical wallcovering.

One book could be all you need to create a focal point wall. Look for old books featuring etchings of animals, botanicals, or another subject you like. Even pages of all text can look chic. Using either the original pages or color copies, hang pages by applying a premixed wallpaper paste to the back of each page using a roller. For the best results, place the first set of pages along the ceiling line and work down from there. Make sure each page is straight, and sweep a wallpaper smoother over each print to take out any wrinkles before moving on to hang the next.

TIP: Try this wallpapering idea using old maps or comic books.

WORLD BOOK

WORLD BOOK

WORLD BOOK

WORLD BOOK

Sit a Spell

Give a thrifted wood folding chair a quick style boost.

A few easy accents lend personal style to a plain-Jane chair. Measure and mark two rows of holes 1 inch apart along the top of the chair. Drill a ⅛-inch hole at each mark, then lace leather cording through the holes to create an X design. Knot ends at the back to secure. Add metal or stenciled numbers to the chairback. To soften the seat, measure the seat size and cut two pieces from an old sweater to fit. With right sides together, sew around pieces, leaving an opening for turning. Insert an outdoor pillow form and hand-stitch opening closed. Treat fabric with water-proofing spray. For a thrifty side table, a garage sale umbrella basket is topped with a glass plate.

TIP: Knit sweaters can unravel when cut and stretch when sewn. Wash old wool sweaters in hot water to felt them before cutting.

Pretty as a Picture

Create living portraits with vintage frames.

Stop by any tag sale or thrift shop and you're sure to stumble upon a handful of old picture frames for a few bucks each. Snatch them up and begin a gallery of natural artwork for a porch or patio space. Give the frame a fresh coat of paint, or if you like the existing patina, let it be. Spray the frame with a clear sealer to protect the finish. If you prefer a weathered look, skip the sealer and let it age with the seasons. Purchase a backless shadowbox or make one from 1×4 boards to fit behind the frame. Attach a picture hanger to the back of the box, and use screws to attach the picture frame to the front of the box. Carefully chip a section from a few small terra-cotta flowerpots. Place potting soil inside the pots and then plant succulents. Hang the frame in a sunny spot and set pots inside.

TIP: Look past what's inside a frame. Some of the best ones may be paired with unsightly artwork or old photos.

Handy Helpers

At home or at the office, put these handy helpers to work.

These projects are made to measure. For the clipboard, remove the clip, cut yardsticks to fit the board, secure with wood glue, clamp, let dry, then replace the clip. Make a small vase by cutting yardsticks and gluing them to a small can. For a fun pencil holder, cut yardsticks to desired size. Drill holes in the corner pieces, and use yarn and a needle to stitch corners together; glue remaining pieces.

TIP: To remove the clipboard clip, drill out the rivets. Reattach the clip using nuts and bolts.

Hang in There

A mix of colorful yardsticks perks up a plain entryway.

Start with a shelf or ledge that fits your space. This little ledge mimics crown molding. Paint the shelf to match one of the yardstick colors and let dry. Cut a piece of plywood the same length of the bottom of the shelf and about 10 inches wide. Cut yardsticks to varying lengths and attach to the board using wood glue, staggering the bottom edges. Clamp and let dry. Attach hanging hardware to the back of the board, then evenly space and install decorative coat hooks across the front. Screw the shelf to the decorated board, and hang on the wall.

Office Space

Small but mighty, this quaint desk doesn't waste space.

Resurrect a broken table as a space-saving workstation. Cut the table in half, or to the desired depth, then saw off the legs. Screw a 1×4 onto the wall, then attach the table to the board using L-shape brackets. Keep pencils and art supplies in check by stashing them in food graters. Just turn the graters upside down and insert a wood or cardboard bottom. Turn an old crib spring into a memo board. If the spring is too large, cut the sides and attach to 1×2s.

Tile Style

Sea glass and paint give this vintage table a fresh look.

This tabletop is a perfect size for trying your hand at mosaic tiling. Create a ¼-inch lip around the table by nailing flexible plastic molding around the perimeter. Paint the table and let dry. Spread premixed adhesive and grout on the tabletop and begin pressing in sea glass pieces, arranging in a predetermined design. Let dry overnight, then grout using adhesive grout and following manufacturer's instructions. Clean all grout from tops of tiles before it dries.

TIP: To help ensure success, dry-fit the sea glass and snap a photo of the design for reference when adhering.

Tiered Treasures

Pair candlesticks and plates to make a sweet serving piece.

Layer your buffet with treats for the eye and the palate. Use glass adhesive to secure a glass candlestick to the bottom of a pretty plate. Repeat with a second candlestick and plate. Use them as individual compotes or stack them with a large plate on the bottom to create a two- or three-level serving tray. You can adhere the candlesticks to the tops of the plates as well, but they are less versatile and harder to store.

TIP: Use mounting putty to secure dishware together while serving, then easily disassemble to store.

Mighty Mini Bar

This petite server works in even the smallest of spaces.

Secondhand shops and flea markets are often teeming with vintage crates. Look for a sturdy one with interesting character and turn it into a rustically beautiful beverage station. Use a jar and pencil to trace scallops onto the front of the crate. Cut along the lines using a jigsaw and a wood blade designed for fine cuts. Sand edges lightly with a sanding block, then drill holes using varied bit sizes. Wipe the crate clean, then stain all sides. Let dry at least 24 hours. Secure a wineglass holder to the underside of the crate, then hang the crate on the wall, nailing into a stud or with secure drywall or masonry anchors.

TIP: When drilling holes, create a template from cardboard to make hole placement easier and more uniform along each scallop.

Winsome Wall Flowers

Help a room bloom with an easy-make display.

To craft this delightful piece, start with a salvaged window frame, preferably with muntins and original hardware for added character. Remove any glass Leave in found condition, or remove hardware, sand smooth, wipe with a tack cloth, and paint desired color. Let dry and reattach hardware. Cut a piece of beaded board or other salvaged wood to fit inside the frame, and attach using finish nails or wood glue. Use old hose nozzles as hooks. Measure and mark placement for each nozzle, drill holes for 1½-inch threaded pipe from a hardware store into the board, then screw a nozzle onto each pipe. Wrap wire or string around the tops of old bottles and hang from the nozzles as petite vases.

TIP: Make a similar display for jewelry, office supplies, or garden tools.

For the Birds

A few new touches turn a pigeon cage into a clever coffee table.

Old wicker and rattan baskets and wood crates are common flea finds, but they typically aren't large enough to fashion into a coffee table. Pigeon crates or baskets, however, are just the right size and offer warm texture and natural appeal to living room spaces. Look for sturdy cages or baskets. Thoroughly wash the piece using a mixture of 1 cup distilled white vinegar and 1 gallon of water. Let dry. Add wood furniture feet or large metal casters under each corner. Depending on the finish, the cage could be stained and sealed or painted. Have a piece of tempered glass cut to fit the top. Leave the cage floor as is or apply pretty wallpaper or ceramic tiles, then use the cage as a display case for collectibles or as extra storage for books or throws.

Make the Rounds

Create a gallery with objects sharing a common theme.

These circular shapes unite to create a unique arrangement and artistic statement. Look for picture frames, mirrors, and various architectural elements of the same shape. Leave them as found or paint or embellish as desired. White paint highlights the intricate detailing on this cast-iron grate, while a gilded picture frame is backed with pink string, woven spiderweb style, to hold decorative cards. A $4 thrift store painting comes to life thanks to paint-pen-embellished forest features. Add hangers to the back if needed.

TIP: To get the arrangement just right, trace each object onto kraft paper and cut out. Tape paper patterns to the wall until you're happy with the design, then hang objects one by one, removing patterns as you go.

Delightful Doilies

Think grandma's doilies are out of vogue? Try this fresh approach.

Collect a slew of old doilies to fit the length of your table and about two doilies wide. Thirty doilies were used for this 7-foot-long table. Hand- or machine-made will do, but select doilies made from natural materials such as cotton to best take the dye. Create various shades of dye by diluting liquid fabric dye in several containers of hot water. Following the manufacturer's instructions, dip the doilies into the dyes until desired colors are achieved, then let dry. Place the doilies on your tabletop and play with the arrangement until you're happy. Each doily should touch the ones around it. Leaving them on the tabletop, hand-stitch the doilies together with matching thread.

TIP: Most vintage doilies are made from cotton, but if you happen across synthetic ones, spray paint them instead of using dye.

Say Cheese

A few fun modifications transform discarded flatware.

Both silver-plate and stainless flatware are easy to find and to work with. To make these cheese markers, place a fork (or spoon) between felt and flatten it in a vise or with a hammer. Mark it using metal stamps and a hammer. Clamp the fork to a work surface and cut the top inch or so off the handle using a rotary tool and cutting disk. Curve the remaining handle by hammering it over a metal dowel using a rubber mallet.

TIP: Darken the stamped letters using black food-safe marker, wiping excess from the surface of the fork.

Found Fixtures

Shine a light on your creativity with these bright ideas.

Lighting can be expensive, so save cash and make a personal statement by converting dome and cylindrical industrial finds—such as metal baskets, copper tins, and metal strainers—into illuminating decor. Use a large drill bit to create a hole in each object wide enough to thread the wiring of a pendant light kit through. Add an Edison bulb and it's lights on!

TIP: Use a table lamp kit to make similar objects into one-of-a-kind table lamps.

Step It Up

Repurpose an old ladder as unique new storage.

This shelving idea flaunts form and function. Cut a wood ladder into two equal sections using a circular saw; sand the cut edges. Cut 1×2 boards for the shelving. Sand, prime, and paint all sides white. On each rung, measure and mark parallel points 4 inches to the right and left of the center. Drill holes at the marks using a countersink drill bit. Attach the top shelf through the holes using 3-inch construction screws. Attach a 1×3 strip of salvaged wood diagonally across the back of the unit, making sure the top shelf is level. Install remaining shelves, then secure the diagonal board into those shelves. Secure a second diagonal board across the back in the opposite direction, mitering it to fit where it meets the first board.

Common Threads

Give traditional embroidery a modern twist.

Save a worn-out rattan chair from the junk pile and use your creativity to give it new life. Remove the old rattan from the seat, and wrap black twine around the seat frame from front to back. Weave contrasting twines under and over the black twine. Sketch a cross-stitch floral design on paper to desired size or print one from online. Using the sketch as a guide and chunky yarns, cross-stitch the design onto the rattan chairback, knotting yarn ends at the back.

TIP: Wrap end of yarn with masking tape to make it easier to thread through rattan.

Pull It All Together

Combine various relics to create clever door pulls.

Search architectural salvage shops for hardware such as these doorknob backplates and water spigot handles to fashion into one-of-a-kind door or drawer knobs. Clean the metal pieces using a stiff wire brush to remove flaking paint or rust. Wipe with a damp cloth and let dry. Prime with a metal primer, then paint, or use a paint specially formulated with rust inhibitors. Let dry. Secure handles on plates using metal adhesive. Top handles off with costume jewelry. We removed the clips from old earrings and secured the pretty baubles to the handles using metal adhesive. When dry, screw finished pieces to the cabinet door.

TIP: For an aged glass look, spray back side of glass doors with Krylon Looking Glass Paint and let dry. Spray with a mixture of vinegar and water, and carefully blot with clean rag to remove bits of paint. Spray a final coat with Looking Glass Paint. Let dry.

Now You're Talking

Fun typography lets wall art speak for itself.

An old window bank salvaged from a garage door nicely frames artwork. A narrow French door or divided glass bifold door also works. Sand the woodwork, then wipe with a tack cloth. Paint with your desired color and let dry. Use screws to attach large bulldog clips at the top center of each glass opening. Find pretty fonts online and print onto canvas sheets (or draw or stencil letters), then hang a sheet from each clip.

TIP: Print words for different seasons or holidays and swap them throughout the year.

INDEX

INDEX